MW01701500

YOUR TIME IS NOW

How to Build Your Dream in the Second Half of Life

Steven E. Kanarian

10-10-10 Publishing

YOUR TIME IS NOW: How to Build Your Dream in the Second Half of Life
www.yourtimenowsecondhalf.com

Paperback ISBN: 978-1-77277-623-2

Publisher
10-10-10 Publishing
Markham, ON Canada

Printed in Canada and the United States of America

Table of Contents

To everyone ready to create their dream lives in their second half of life, may your journey be made clear through the pages of this book.

I appreciate Bill McCabe's friendship and shared interest in writing. Bill has been a friend through thick and thin and we are there for each other through the good and challenging moments.

Kevin Bachi has always supported and encouraged us during our endeavors. Kevin is a kindred soul in doing the right thing and pushing the envelope. Kevin showed me the beauty of Maine and Nubble Lighthouse. Kevin is a unique individual, my best man, and most notably packed his bags and started coming to New York City on September 11, 2001, when he could not reach me or Carl by cellular phone.

I appreciate the support and guidance from Mary Burton when I was a young paramedic in New York City. Mary was appropriately named Mother Mary Queen of Paramedics by Jimmy Booth. Mary would give us advice and keep us on the straight and narrow. Mary was a living example of emotional intelligence before any of us knew what it was. A conversation with Mary changed my life and prepared me to meet and marry Moira, the love of my life.

I could not mention everybody who helped me learn and pushed me to improve. I appreciate all those who were a positive force and even some whose negativity inspired me to prove them wrong and succeed.

Acknowledgments

I want to acknowledge those in my life that have helped me achieve the level of success and happiness I have reached.

I want to thank Noah St. John for his inspiration to be a life coach, author, and speaker. Noah St. John encouraged me to follow my passion of helping people and sharing wisdom with clients like he has, being a Hay House author and speaker.

I want to thank Marianne Lepre-Nolan, who has been a great cheerleader in my journey dealing with life. Marianne has supported me in reaching my coaching goals and publishing this book. Marianne has expanded my understanding of the heights to which coaching can take one.

I want to thank my wife, Moira, for her loving support in reaching our dream of having a loving family and a successful life. Moira was an unstoppable servant of the people. Moira served New York City, her family, her community, and God. Moira did everything with energy and her love of life. I appreciate her support and strength, which allowed me to pursue my career and have a wonderful family. Moira was a special person and the love of my life, who I was blessed to be with for twenty-six years. May she rest in peace and feel satisfaction.

I thank my mother, Mary Zahm, for allowing us to dream and follow our path in life. My mother often helped me with writing assignments at the eleventh hour. Who knew I would one day grow up to write books?

I want to thank my father, Peter Kanarian, who provided us with a great home in rural Massachusetts. My father taught us to appreciate family, education, and travel. Growing up in Massachusetts, I learned to do the hard things and never give up. These skills allowed me to succeed as a New York City paramedic for twenty-five years and a September 11, 2001, rescuer.

I want to thank my children, Alex, Theresa, and Michael, who continue to amaze and impress me with their uniqueness and success. I once thought that children grow up reflecting their parents and would be similar. I am amazed at how our children take these special qualities and blend them in with their uniqueness. I look forward to being a part of your awesome lives.

My uncle, Thomas Westgate, is a shining example of how a person can set new goals and strive for excellence in work and sports.

Don Faeth taught me to question what I know to be true and try new paths. His influence has enhanced my life and joy.

I want to thank my good friend and mentor, Jason Hums, who helped me "turn the lid of the jar a few turns" when I was flat in my career. Jason introduced me to teaching and has been a partner in success as we both rose to our levels of success.

Foreword

Are you putting off your goals and creating your dream life, assuming you will get to it eventually? I am here to tell you that tomorrow never comes, and you run the risk of reaching retirement with a bucket list of dreams and goals that are still unfulfilled.

Your Time Is Now: How to Build Your Dream in the Second Half of Life is the solution you have been waiting for! With practical tips and guidance, Steven Kanarian helps you to create your dream life in your second half.

Every chapter focuses on different areas of achieving your goals and dreams, from your values to your vision. Steven also offers common sense advice on how to identify and address potential obstacles that can pop up as you work to create the life of your dreams.

Your Time Is Now offers a life coach and cheerleader, as Steven shares his story of having to switch gears after retiring from being a first responder. No matter where you are in life, Steven can help you to create your vision and then bring it to life.

Your Time Is Now: How to Build Your Dreams in the Second Half of Life is a guidebook for building support, defining your goals, and taking charge of your life. Achieve the satisfaction of a bucket list of memories by taking charge of your life right now!

Raymond Aaron
***New York Times* Bestselling Author**

Chapter 1

Why It's Your Time Now!

Life has a way of slipping by quickly as we go through its various stages. We grow up with interests and hobbies. We have an idea of what kind of career success we want. Later, we get married and raise children. Years go by, you build a career, raise your family, and before you know it, retirement is staring you in the face. Your kids have grown, you have reached a level of success, and now you ask yourself, "What is next?" You look to rekindle that spark with your partner and plan a great life for the second half of your life.

When you were a teenager, there was likely a list of dreams and plans of everything you wanted to experience throughout your life. There were activities and hobbies you did for sheer enjoyment. I enjoyed playing hockey on a pond in rural Massachusetts, built models, and dreamed of one day being a firefighter. My friends and I would play football and re-create the success of the Pittsburgh Steelers in the mud and rain.

Growing into adulthood and succeeding can be satisfying. Still, falling into a routine is easy, and before you know it, you wonder where the time went. "Someday" has become your life's mantra, which means many of those dreams and visions of your future have been put on indefinite hold.

Many of us have battled to hang onto hope, but we also have a clearer understanding of how short life can be and the importance of seizing the day because tomorrow is not guaranteed. As a former New York City Fire Department (FDNY) paramedic, I have a special understanding of how fleeting life can be. Lives can be cut short in the blink of an eye, with many things left undone.

Time passes while we work and take care of our families. How often have you changed plans from golfing, hiking, or spending the weekend at the beach because of family functions? You know you're doing the right thing for your family and applying the value of "family first," which is important, but your desire to develop your passion lingers in the back of your mind.

I measured my success as a father by the number of hugs and smiles I received from my kids. The song "Cat's in the Cradle" by Harry Chapin always provided a chance to sit back and ask myself, "Am I becoming the person who sings that song? Am I being a good father and husband? How can I lead a balanced work and family life?"

Work can be satisfying and a means to a great life. The time required to work and commute erodes time with family. I can remember coming home from my job as a paramedic in the FDNY and being exhausted. We use our energy for our jobs and come home on an empty emotional tank, leaving little for our families. I tried to make up for it by being present on weekends and at school band and sporting events. Holidays sometimes had to be delayed because I was working. I always felt my kids should know you have to work and apply yourself to be successful. There is a cost and many lost opportunities when working in emergency services.

When you get that promotion, care for a parent, or support your kids in school sports, it can seem like you are delaying the dream to the second half of your life. Every dream and goal is somewhere in the future, and that means what is happening in the present is less important than the future you are imagining and dreaming about. You really only have to worry about today. Put off things that can be delayed and make the most of today.

The challenge for many of us is that we have built routines and followed well-defined paths for our lives, only to reach retirement years and realize there is so much that is still undone. Routines are great for processes we do every day. However, it is important to review our life's routines in light of our goals and the vision for the life we love. You can begin to align your life with your dreams by following your values and vision of retirement.

Retirement does not mean that your life is over and you are riding off into the sunset, but it does mean that you have to figure out how you want to spend this second half of life. The time is now to start building your dream life.

Take the time to map out and envision your ideal life. What would a typical day look like? Would it be filled with meaningful work that inspires you, or would you be exploring parts of the world that have always fueled your imagination? Would it involve spending more time with family and friends, creating more memories that you all will cherish? Think about the sights, sounds, and smells of this ideal life. How does it feel to walk on the beach in the Caribbean? How does the ocean smell? What birds do you hear? Have you seen the Bahama warbler or the pileated woodpecker?

Perhaps you have seen a need in your community but have never been in a position to do something about it. Your ideal life might include creating a program and throwing your time and energy into efforts that benefit your community far beyond what you have been able to accomplish in your role as a first responder.

No matter what type of life you dream of, that dream is the blueprint that can help you make choices and changes in the present to achieve it. Action is a key part of creating the life of your dreams. Too often, we dream it but tend to trip up on the obstacles we envision are making our dreams impossible.

Focusing on those obstacles, whether real or imaginary, can end up becoming a blockade in its own right. Simply put, our minds and the obstacles we visualize can end up stopping us before we even get started. That leaves dreams unfulfilled and our lives not meeting what we had expected or hoped for as our future. Movement will occur when you create your vision of your ideal life. Once your mind believes in the dream, movement will occur and realign the obstacles to make room for opportunity.

Starting out to create a meaningful life for yourself in this second half of life means identifying all the mental roadblocks that have actually stopped your dreams from coming to fruition. Those mental blocks can include self-doubt, a lack of confidence in your abilities, or even struggling to overcome the negative voices from the past about inadequacy or not being good enough, which were programmed in your mind by well-meaning people who wanted to keep you safe and in your lane. Later, we will be diving into identifying obstacles and the resources necessary to overcome them.

Your second half of life doesn't have limits, but too often, we create limits on ourselves, imagining that our dreams are meant to stay in the dream world and never become part of our reality. I am here to tell you that your dreams are possible, that nothing is completely out of reach. But before you can start making changes in your life, you need to get motivated.

In physics, an object will stay at rest until acted upon by some force. Once it is in motion, then it will stay in motion until another force acts upon it. Right now, you are at the point where you need to stop being the object at rest and get in motion. Take action to get yourself moving in the direction of the life you want to live.

Building the Second Half of Your Life

Still, determining where you are going to put your energy right now can be overwhelming. You might have a list of places that you want to travel to, but you struggle with trying to figure out how to begin. The costs can appear so extensive that you feel ready to give up. Then there are the realities of traveling to areas where you don't speak the language or don't understand the customs. That level of doubt about your abilities can leave you with a passport that has no stamps in it.

On the other hand, you might want to start a new business venture, but you worry that you don't have the skills to manage it or that you don't have the capital to get the business off the ground. Then there are the issues with learning how to market your business, working with social media, and so much more. It seems like too big a risk to take, especially when you are so close to retirement.

Perhaps you want to get more involved in the community but are not sure where your talents could be put to good use. There might be multiple opportunities and you are so excited about them all. How do you narrow it down, allowing you to use your time effectively?

You might also see multiple needs within the community where your talents could be helpful. You can end up feeling like the young boy in the fairy tale, who just kept trying to plug the leaks in a dam, but more leaks continued to appear. You are just one person, and it seems like it is more than you are able or willing to juggle.

These are just a few examples, but as you can see, it is easy to come up with obstacles or reasons why you can't do it. It becomes paralyzing, so your motivation is stifled. Our brains, when they become overwhelmed, simply shut down and we end up doing nothing at all.

When those challenges and obstacles stack up, then your present situation might seem like the safe bet and the best way to live your second act. Inaction becomes your choice as you avoid the options in front of you. But is it really the best if you are not satisfied or your dreams are left on a shelf?

Another challenge you might face is not knowing how the second act will turn out. I love watching football games, but my favorite ones are where the score is close and the two teams are battling it out for victory. One team falls behind, and the moves they make in the second half of the game will determine if they go home with a win or a loss.

Right now, you are facing that same sense of urgency. The choices you make right now are going to determine how your second half will turn out. But there are fears that come up. You might have a fear of losing, fear of missing out, fear of succeeding, or a fear of the unknown.

Overcoming all these fears can be tricky. Fear can end up stifling your courage and make you wonder if it wouldn't be better to just leave things as they are. Let your dreams stay in your imagination, instead of giving them height, depth, and breadth. And that is when the fear wins, and you start building a list of regrets.

After all, the life you have now might not be what you want, but it is what you know. There is comfort in the familiar, but that doesn't mean that the familiar is the best for you. The leap into the unknown is not easy to take, but it can lead to some of the best experiences and relationships of our lives. Your life as you know it will be different because you decide to take a leap, and that might be uncomfortable initially. But what you get in return will be worth it.

There is going to be hard work and effort involved. Nothing in life ever comes without it. Your successes were because you put in the effort and the hard work, knowing that it would allow you to turn your goals into reality. But what is interesting is that as you put in the hard work, the doors of opportunity started opening in ways that you never expected.

Taking the Snap! The Second Half of Life

Life is like a football game, and the clock is running. You only have so much time to make plays and achieve your goal of winning the game. Football games have stages of storming, gaining momentum, and achieving victory. Early in the game, teams are trying to establish rhythm and dominance. Often, in the second half, the losing team will get a sense of urgency and rally to win the game. Teams will rally to play hard even when they know they cannot win. They rally, despite overwhelming odds, to preserve their honor and prove their worth.

Like a football game, we spend the first half using our time but not appreciating that time is limited. Later, we realize we have more days behind us than in front of us. Unfortunately, we really do not know how long our lives will be. We have to enjoy each day and make long-term plans to do the things we want, according to our values and desires.

In Super Bowl LI, the Patriots found themselves losing the game after the first half. The idea of losing the Super Bowl was unimaginable to the Patriots. Julian Edelman spoke during the halftime break, saying, "We got this; let's get out there and finish this thing."

In the second half, the Patriots had difficulties but soon found their rhythm through the vision of winning and taking deliberate action. A reception here, an interception to get the ball back, and gradually the Patriots overcame a 28-to-3-point deficit to win the game. You, too, can have your own second half victory celebration by creating your vision and taking deliberate action.

The truth is that all of us are getting older, and that comes with its own set of challenges. You end up having to juggle new health issues while still managing your finances effectively, particularly when it seems that everything is going up except your retirement accounts. When we delay in the game of life, the penalties are wondering what could have been if we had stepped out and made a change.

When I coach different individuals, I find that they are often struggling with taking their first step. They might even have some idea of what they want to do in their second act but are unclear about how to begin. It takes courage to start down a new path or make significant changes to your life. Stoking that courage can often be the most critical step that you take, because that courage will help you to act. Once you take your first steps, then your excitement can begin to grow, and your motivation will drive you forward.

Right now, I need you to stand up to the power of inertia and embrace the courage it takes to go after your dreams and turn them into your reality. I need you to recognize that you deserve to take this step and make a change. You have done for others, sacrificed for your family, built a career, and now it is time to embrace your dreams and bring them to life.

How can you overcome your inertia and fear? Start by looking at all you have been able to accomplish up to this point. Honestly, it is impressive. You have cared for your family, built your career, created and nurtured relationships that have added joy to your life, built a support system, and likely volunteered to some degree in your community. You have already built an impressive legacy, but it doesn't need to end just because you are transitioning to the next phase of your life.

"Not all who wonder or wander are lost."
– Bear McCreary

The reason you need to look at all you have accomplished up to this point is because you will realize how much you have achieved. We tend to forget our successes and dwell on our failures. It will help you see that you are capable of building an amazing second act, especially when you realize how impressive the first act has been.

As a New Yorker, theatre, plays, and Broadway musicals are a part of this city's DNA. Many plays are divided into two or three acts. The first and second acts are all about setting up the story, identifying the characters, and helping you as the audience to understand their challenges. Then comes the third act, which is often the most exciting. Problems are resolved and you root for the characters to succeed and get their happy ending. For the playwright and the actors, their goal is to leave the audience entertained as the curtain comes down on the third act.

Your next act is beginning right now. You are the playwright, determining where the story turns next. Unlike being a member of the audience at a play, you have the power to determine how the story goes and where the main character ends up. You are writing your next act right now and it can be amazing!

Over the next few chapters, I am going to talk about some of the obstacles you might face and how you can overcome them to achieve incredible results. I am going to share some of my life experiences, including how you can use your second act to continue to grow. Learning never stops unless we choose to let it stop.

Let's explore what your next act can look like and how the choices you make right now can help build that amazing future by clarifying your values. Whether you know it or not, your values are the foundation of how you make decisions. As you will soon find out, your decisions now are critical to redesigning your future to match the dreams in your head.

Chapter 2

Clarifying Your Values Outline

Did you know that every decision starts with your values and priorities? It can be hard to imagine when you are walking through the grocery store and choosing what mustard or salad dressing to buy, but your values are coming into play. In choosing the store brand mustard, your values regarding money and how it should be spent are coming to the forefront of your decision making. But you might choose that national brand dressing because the company has a focus on sustainability that you appreciate.

Prioritizing how you are going to spend your time often comes down to your values, which play a role in your decision making, even if you don't always realize it. Values are a crucial part of living your life with purpose and setting fulfilling goals because they are the qualities that are most meaningful to us. The values that we cherish are often the ones that get us through the struggles and challenges that we face throughout our lives. Values are the guideposts that tell us which way to go in life and how to make our decisions.

Today, society's values have shifted to being more materialistic, focusing on getting famous, buying the latest gadgets, and striving for success in your career. The pandemic was a chance for many families to slow down and reevaluate how they are spending their time and energy. The last few years have been a value check and, truthfully, opened our eyes to how little we were investing in our relationships with our families and friends.

Connecting and aligning to your values is a boost to your courage, your self-discovery, and your self-development. But to truly understand your values, it is essential that you understand what helped you to form them in the first place.

Where Do We Get Our Values?

Every value you cherish now has its roots in your life experiences, but those life experiences are greatly impacted by our cultures. Values are imposed when we are young as part of our parent's efforts to shape our morality and ethics. Think about the values of care/harm, fairness/cheating, loyalty/betrayal, and authority/subversion. Each of these pairs is malleable, but you can easily see how they also inform our political leanings and what we each perceive as being "right or wrong."

While the values that your parents tried to instill through their life lessons were geared toward promoting the good, that good is defined according to their culture and background.

Religious beliefs, for example, can easily demonstrate how the divide between one culture and another is created. When you look at the laws of any country, you see how specific values are encoded into their laws. Most countries, for example, have clear laws against murder, assault, or other forms of abuse. Yet, their religious and cultural beliefs play a large role in defining assault, murder, and abuse.

Clearly, the values you use to define what is right or wrong, to determine the best way to handle a situation at work or within your family, start within our families and early cultural experiences. Those values are reinforced throughout our lives.

The value of kindness, for instance, is imposed by our parents but then reinforced at our schools. When you apply the value of kindness, it helps to create greater social bonds with your friends and classmates. Adapting to be kind to others is often rewarded, while being mean is often punished. The values we are indoctrinated with as children, from our parents and culture, become the lens through which we view and make judgments about the world. The challenge is that as our experiences grow, the values of our early childhood might no longer resonate the same way.

That can make critical decisions more challenging. While we still want to participate in the society in which we grew up, its shared reality, built by customs and activities meant to give us purpose and significance, may no longer fit who we are or what we see as important.

Culture impacts our values because it describes appropriate behavior for multiple situations, with the goal of helping you get along with those around you. Travel to a different country and you'll see what I mean. In China, they elevate the group and family over the individualism that appears to be bred into us as Americans. Go to Hawaii and see how relaxation and balance are elevated over a work-oriented culture, often found in major metro areas throughout the United States.

It is not that the values of one country are better than another, but they clearly show that while we might believe our values are rock-solid, the truth is that they can be fluid as we change cultures and collect various life experiences. Where things get muddy is when competing values are also competing for supremacy. After all, if all values are seeking the good, then how can we say one is greater than another or that one needs more of our energy than another?

Values Are the Guideposts of Our Journey

We make decisions along the way by applying our values. Some people make decisions based on selfishness or opportunity. Balanced people make decisions based on their values. The trouble comes when values are conflicting with one another. It can be easy to slip into the mindset of right/wrong and make judgments accordingly.

When someone tells you that your values are wrong, your mind immediately starts to block them out. You can't hear what they are saying anymore, because you are ready to defend the values that define who you are, your culture, and how you grew up.

Here's a different way to look at it. Consider looking at competing values from a better or worse perspective. This exercise allows you to acknowledge the virtues of another person's values, while also recognizing that some values should be elevated above others. By doing this, you can create some common ground, recognizing that both of you are coming into the discussion with values that can advance the situation.

Plus, when you are thinking in terms of better or worse, you aren't getting personal. It becomes a discussion about how the values impact the public sphere, including how they impact others, and the consequences of those values when they are fully implemented in your daily life.

A great example is when missionaries came to foreign tribes with the goal of converting them, bringing food and supplies meant to make their lives better. However, they also brought diseases that devastated the villages. When looking at the consequences, it becomes clear that there must be a better alternative to advance the value of generosity and compassion than the missionaries bringing disease.

Value judgments should not be confused with moralistic judgments, since value judgments reflect our beliefs on how life can best be served, but moralistic judgments are made based on the behaviors of others that fail to support our value judgments. When it comes to articulating your values and using them to guide your decisions, be sure that you are voicing your value without classifying or making a moral judgment of someone else.

Now, let's take this understanding of values and put it into perspective with trying to create your ideal life. Likely, defining your ideal life is going to depend heavily on the values that have already characterized your life to date. When you analyze your values, do you find that they naturally align with making your life better, or are they counterintuitive to your dreams and goals for yourself?

Watershed Decision

A watershed decision is made by applying your values and decision-making ability to a life-defining decision. It is at this moment when you have to decide whether your values need to change to better reflect where you want to go and the person you want to be, or if your values are accurately reflecting you now and in the future.

Too often, we don't take the time to understand how we came to a decision. Instead, we just quickly gather facts and then decide, not recognizing how much our values have played into the process. But when it comes to deciding upon the vision of your ideal life, you need to have a deeper understanding of the role of your values.

Are values an obstacle for your dreams in the second half of life? Your values reflect what you find meaningful, leading you away from short-term satisfaction to long-term fulfillment. Our values play a role in how well we thrive in life, but we don't have to look far to find them. Rather than being created, it is a journey of discovery.

The truth is that your values are going to drip down into your beliefs, behaviors, and decisions. If you are unclear about your values, then it can be difficult to determine the best direction for your life. Your values are a form of intrinsic motivation, which can be powerful when it comes to moving yourself toward a goal or a dream. After all, obstacles are likely to make themselves apparent as you work to achieve your ideal life. The question is whether your values will keep you motivated to work through those obstacles to create a meaningful and valuable life for yourself.

Your core values are the central part of your existence. Think of a seed sprouting. There is a place within us where our core values are from, the ones that reside in our hearts, helping us to shape who we are and what we are meant to become.

If you feel your values do not align with your vision for your dream, I would suggest revising your dream so that you are in alignment with your values. Misalignment will result in dissatisfaction, stress, and unhappiness. If you feel misaligned, it can also be a good time to access your values. The truth is that as we age and have a broader range of experiences, our personal values can also shift. A personal value is what the words mean to you when you describe a specific value. For instance, you might value integrity. The feelings, pictures, and motivations that you associate with integrity make up your personal value.

What is interesting is that our values do not operate individually but more as a unique network. There is plenty of overlap, as values often connect themselves to each other in a variety of ways. Let's take integrity for a moment. It can often be interlinked with truth, honesty, and courage of your convictions. Notice that values tend to support each other, becoming a foundation of what you find valuable and meaningful in your life.

Therefore, don't be quick to assume that the personal values you hold now will always be that way. Let's do an exercise that can help you to define your core and personal values, as well as the results that come from implementing your values in your life.

Understanding your values is the best foundation for your second act. Your core values are often what shape your dreams, because you dream about what brings you joy and meaning. There are many dreams that you quickly discard, simply because they don't align with who you are.

One of my core values was a desire to help others. As a result, I ended up being a first responder in New York City, assisting people in some of their worst moments. Being a first responder is both inspiring and overwhelming. Eventually, I realized that it was time to find another way to help others. Coaching is my dream for the second half of my life, because it allows me to assist others in reaching their dreams. Although my ideal life has changed, what is meaningful to me hasn't changed at all.

Clearly, your values will help you to make choices that get you closer to your ideal life. If you make choices for a dream that isn't consistent with what you find meaningful, then you won't find that dream being as amazing as you thought.

Your dreams should always be consistent with your values. That level of alignment brings satisfaction on many levels. However, when that alignment is lacking, obstacles start to spring up and you can easily get frustrated because you aren't making any progress to achieving your ideal life. If you find that obstacles are regularly creeping up and slowing your progress, then examine your values and your dreams closely. You might find that the alignment is not there, and adjustments have to be made, either to your values or your goals. You will know in your heart when your dream matches your life purpose.

When I graduated from paramedic training, I was faced with a watershed decision. I was working in Massachusetts as an EMT and was going to work as a paramedic after graduation. I received an acceptance letter from the New York City Emergency Medical Service on the day of graduation. Which one would I choose? I first thought I would stay in Massachusetts and get a good medic job instead of heading to New York, but I agonized over the choice. Finally, I listened to my friend Kevin and decided to stay in Massachusetts. The day of the final medical interview, I sat up in my bed at five a.m., my heart pounding, and I thought about the choice. I decided to go to the medical interview in Queens, NY, and take the job. I knew in my heart it was the courageous decision. It felt good.

This decision was made over time considering my life's purpose and desire to prove myself on a grand stage. This decision took me to a wild and rewarding career in New York City. I met great friends and my wife. Together, Moira and I had a wonderful family. I worked in the Bronx in the 1980s and saved lives. I even had the opportunity to walk on the pages of American history on September 11, 2001.

With that in mind, let's talk about how you might have drifted away from your dreams and how you can get back on track.

Chapter 3

Remind Yourself of Your Dream

We all had an ideal life in our minds in our twenties. But then we started building our careers and having families. The next thing you know, you are in your late forties and wondering where the time has gone. Your dream has cobwebs on it. As you are reading this, look around at where your life currently stands.

Your routine is based on the habits you have created over a lifetime. Those habits helped you to support your kids, take care of your parents, and manage your career. The hamster wheel of career and family kept you running around managing every aspect of life for everyone else, and that can start to feel overwhelming and frustrating.

If one of your loved ones is dealing with an illness, on top of everything else that life is throwing your way, then you are also managing endless doctor appointments, prescriptions, and therapies, all while trying to make ends meet. There seems to be little time or energy for anything that you want or dream of accomplishing.

But now things are beginning to shift in your life. Your children are heading off to college or the workforce. The care of your parents might have transitioned to a facility or even just a more balanced division of labor among your siblings. Now, it is time to return your focus to you and your dreams. How will you live the second half of your life?

Shake Yourself Out of Your Routine

Right now, it is time to shake up your routine. The habits of a lifetime have kept your family on track, but are they still serving you? It might be that your routine has gone from being helpful to keeping you trapped in a comfortable zone, but not one that is moving you closer to your goals and dreams.

Perhaps at this point, you might be thinking, "I am not even sure I remember what my dream life was." Your routine has become a trap. Here is what you need to do. Shake up that routine. Try taking a risk, stepping out of the same things every day.

That could involve making a different choice in your career or making changes in your lifestyle that give you more freedom to explore your interests and the things that bring you joy. It might be a little scary to break away from your routine. You might feel like the whole world will come crashing down if you shift your routine, but that is not the case.

Instead, shaking up your routine can be a great way to get excited again about what the future holds and the possibilities that are within your reach. So, what are a few ways that you can shake up your routine? Surprisingly enough, it can be something as small as driving a different way to work. When you do that, then you might be surprised at what you see that can spark your creativity. Changing up your look or even rekindling a new relationship can be some changes that get you jumpstarted to see things differently. Why not try a different restaurant or take a trip to a random city in the USA. I recommend Key West, Maine, and San Diego.

I have found that traveling gives you an opportunity to get out of your mouse-maze of life and get a feel for what you want to do in life. I started working as a paramedic in New York City in 1984. I took my first vacation a year later. I flew to Jamaica on a cold, gray day out of Kennedy Airport. The sun was shining brightly after we flew above the clouds. I learned the sun is always shining; you just have to lift your mindset above the clouds. I will never forget the look of the clear, azul-colored water and seeing the stained wooden boats in the Caribbean Ocean as we approached Jamaica. I knew then, at that moment, the Caribbean stirs my soul and would always be a part of my life moving forward.

Once you have shaken up your routine, you are going to feel more energized. That energy is key to dreaming big, visualizing your ideal life through the lens of your values. Remember, you want to align your dreams with what you find meaningful. But don't limit your dreams to what you believe is possible.

Now is the time to dream in 3-D, with vivid color. But why might you be struggling to identify your dream life?

Dreaming Is Not Only for the Young

The problem with society today is that dreams are associated with young people. We ask them what they want to do with their lives, and we try to figure out how we can support them in reaching their dreams. But rarely do we ask the same of those who are older, who have raised families and built businesses or careers. But in the midst of doing all that work, you have forgotten to keep dreaming.

"A winner is a dreamer who never gives up."
– Nelson Mandela

Your dreams have been put on the shelf for so long that they have essentially become forgotten. Now is the time for you to get the dust rag out and rediscover what inspired you in the past. What did you want to accomplish in your life? You are not too old to figure it out, and you are definitely not too old to pursue it.

Never allow your age to be an excuse for not trying to achieve your ideal life. You should not accept your life as it is, because if you do, then you might find yourself living with a bunch of regrets. No one ever wants to get to the end of their life and be spending time dealing with regrets.

Instead, let's focus on making some incredible memories—no excuses that "what you want is impossible, so there is no point in going after those dreams." I want you to dream big and never say that you are too old or it is too late, because neither of those things is true. Success might not always come when you want it, but that doesn't mean success is only limited to a select few young ones.

"I believe it's important to stay young at heart, to have faith in what might seem impossible, and to have goals beyond your current abilities or temporary means."
– Hayley Williams

You need to be willing to devote your life to your dreams and goals with consistent work and manifestation. That might be easier said than done, but here are just a few examples that I believe can inspire you to keep shaking up your routine and dreaming big.

Samuel L. Jackson is one of the A-list Hollywood actors. His voice and face are icons, but he didn't get his big break until he was 43, when he appeared in Spike Lee's *Jungle Fever*. Julia Child actually worked in advertising for most of her life, but at the age of 50, she released her first cookbook. When she finally passed away, Julia was known as one of the original celebrity chefs.

But not only are you not too old to pursue your dreams, you can change your dreams. Vera Wang is known for her work in the fashion industry, but she actually dreamed of being an Olympic figure skater. Once that dream failed, she didn't assume that success had passed her by. Instead, she dived into the world of fashion at age 40 and has become one of the leaders in the industry.

Your dreams could be starting a new business, exploring the world, learning new skills, or even going after the causes that you are passionate about. The dreams you have now can be informed by what you have already experienced in your life. Perhaps you found a way to improve a process or address a need in your community. The point is that your dream can be as big as your imagination. It doesn't have to be limited just because you have a few decades under your belt.

My Dream of Moving to NYC to Be a Paramedic

When you achieve your dream, I can honestly tell you that it ends up being greater than what you imagined was possible. The dream ends up being greater than you set out to achieve, just because of the unexpected challenges and who you become along the way. The challenge that you might have is that you achieved many of your dreams and goals up to this point, but now that you are ready to enter the next stage, you might be unsure what to do or what your next big dream is.

I always dreamed of being a firefighter. I read the history of the fire service and major fires that changed history. There were no entrance exams being given for departments when I graduated high school. I was told to take first aid and CPR classes. I took those classes and then became an instructor. Next, I took the emergency medical technician class. Eventually, I realized emergency medical services was where the action and challenges were. I set my sights on the biggest city in our country and was hired in 1984 by the New York City Emergency Medical Service, which was later merged with FDNY. Little did I know that I would respond to the attack on the World Trade Center and walk on the pages of American history.

When I retired from the FDNY, that was the first time I didn't have a driving passion. Like many of us, I faced the challenge of figuring out what was next. My family was in a different place, and my career with the FDNY was over. You might know exactly what I am talking about. The future is filled with unknowns, and that can be scary. I found the team I worked with and the important work we did as paramedics was gone. "How will I fill that void?" I asked myself. I was lacking a sense of purpose.

When you focus on your dreams, you take control of the direction of your life, and the future can be less frightening. However, I don't want you to pick a dream based on the practical concerns of life, like how big the salary is or how many hours you have to work. It needs to be something that you love to do. This might have been a dream that was pushed to the side for more practical reasons, but now that you have the time and ability, you need to focus on yourself. You need to find something you are passionate about. How do you fulfill your life and live within your values?

If you are struggling to find your dream, start by making a list of everything that you love to do. Don't focus on whether you can make money from it or not. Just lay out everything that brings you joy. What activity puts wind in your sail? As you start to write, you might be reminded of the dreams that you pushed to the side, simply because you didn't have time or other priorities came up.

As a parent, for instance, your children become the priority. So, if a dream or goal of yours takes time away from them and their needs, you might end up postponing it or just deciding that it wasn't meant to be.

But times have changed! You are now in a place in your life where you can think about what you want. How do you want the second half of your life to look? What do you want to explore and discover? The great thing about taking risks and having new experiences is what it teaches us about ourselves. Be open to trying new things, and don't count yourself out because of your age or society's expectations about what middle-aged people do.

While you are making the list of everything you love to do, give yourself quiet time to contemplate what brings you joy. It can be easy to leave things out when you are rushing around the house or trying to think with all the noise of the daily routine. My advice is to try waking up a little earlier than the rest of the family, so you can have reflection time for yourself. Yes, it might be easier to roll over and hit the snooze button, but that won't help you define your dreams and give them a voice.

Find Your Quiet Place

You should have a favorite spot, one that brings you peace every time you are there. Your quiet spot may be a quiet room in the house, a seat at your library, or a favorite museum. I like hiking in Harriman State Park and challenging myself. I find exercise gets the creative juices flowing. Use that time to just breathe, letting go of your stress. Write down your ideas and thoughts as they come to you. Don't be quick to censor yourself. This point of the process is about letting your imagination and creativity fly free.

Walking is a good way to get away and think. Meandering around the neighborhood can help you to clear your head, while stepping away from the noise and constant chaos that seems to always fill your life at home. That walk won't be full of the demands of your routine, so enjoy it and let your mind and heart relax. The ideas that come out of this peaceful time can give you a better definition of your dream and what you want your ideal life to look like. I enjoy long walks and often walk the seven miles from the car dealer to my home to get exercise and quiet time.

At this stage of building your dream, don't get stuck on how you are going to accomplish your dreams or create that ideal life. Before you can create a map to get there, you need to know where you are heading. My parents would take us on family trips and, of course, they would pull out the big atlas. My mom or dad would map out the route before we even left, so they knew what highways we would travel and the various exits we would need to take. Yes, I am a map person. I use GPS but love the feel of a map and the detail they give.

The work you do right now is about deciding on the destination, not necessarily the route. We will get to that later.

Dream Building Exercise: 1

For two minutes, sit down and write the things you loved to do as a child. This is a no-judgment zone, so write down everything in your mind.

1.____

2.____

3.____

4.____

5.____

Dream Building Exercise: 2

Write down the things you would love to do in your second half of life; think big, and don't worry about "the how."

"Your desires point in the direction of your life purpose."
– Stacy Morgenstern

Your dream for the second half of life is a work in progress that you can add or subtract anytime. Nothing is set in stone. Like your parents on the road trip, the route can change for various reasons. Construction, detours, and more can mean that your route has to be altered. But for now, the goal is to decide on a destination.

You will be amazed at how the universe will bring you what you want and how the steps to take to acquire your dream will become clear. Your job is to visualize what you want so that the process of defining your second half can begin.

Review the list of things you loved to do as a child and teen. Then think of the thing you would like to do in the second half of your life. Don't be practical. Think big!

1.____

2.____

3.____

4.____

5.____

Chapter 4

Visualizing Your Dream

As a kid, imagination and dreaming are considered necessary. We achieve nothing in the world without first dreaming about it. Think about how you encouraged your children to create through drawing, music, or storytelling. In each instance, as they explained that drawing, sang that song, or told you the amazing story with all the heroes, you applauded and encouraged them to use their imagination.

Even if you didn't realize it at the time, when you asked them what they wanted to be when they grew up, you were helping them to visualize their future, to give it the types of details necessary to see themselves on that firetruck or in that rocket blasting off to space.

So, while you are a child, you are encouraged to dream and visualize an amazing future without limits, fostering your creativity in many ways. I don't know when exactly the switch happens, but somewhere around middle school, the focus shifts to what will make us the most money, what career is practical, and putting limits on what we can do and who we can be. When you look at the side of the road, where does your car go? It naturally goes where your eyes are focused. Naturally, the car veers to where you are looking when you are driving. The same is true for our lives. They are shaped by what we focus on.

When I was a paramedic, I would be frustrated by mediocrity and some people's desire to just get by. I would tell my partners, "We are eagles, so keep your chin up and soar into the sky. Don't look down when you're flying."

When it comes to creating your dream life, you need to be careful where your thoughts go, because distractions can shift your thoughts and take you away from where you want to go. You can reach your goals by keeping your focus on what you want and avoiding distractions that can take you off course.

Too often, as adults, we forget how to dream big, visualize, and, most importantly, be creative. You have become the adult who focuses on responsibilities instead of what you want, and your dreams have become dusty, sitting on a shelf in your mind. Being practical becomes a limitation, telling us the dream isn't possible because we are too old or don't have enough money.

Those limitations shape the rest of our lives and often leave us with regrets about opportunities we bypassed to stay on the safe path. We start to believe our dreams are not possible to achieve and so we simply stop trying.

When you go to the circus, you see a large elephant attached to a pole by a simple rope. Even though it is clear that he could pull the post out and walk away, the elephant never does. A gentleman asked the trainer why the elephant stayed by the pole. The trainer said, "When they are small, we tie them to the pole, and they can't pull it out. As they grow and get older, they simply stop trying because they don't think it is possible."

Are you the elephant? Have you stopped trying, even though you are strong enough and capable of achieving your dreams?

I want to coach you through those limitations that you have set upon yourself. Instead of focusing your energy on why it won't work or isn't possible, let's shift that energy toward building and visualizing this next chapter of your life. I want you to get excited because there are so many possibilities. It's time to embrace your inner child and dream big. You can achieve what the mind believes!

"Do not look at the pigeons on the ground; fly like an eagle."
– Steven Kanarian

What is your dream? Could it be starting your own business or living in a different country? Could it be going back to school or setting your artistic side free? Your dream is as unique as you are.

Take a minute and write down some thoughts about your dream life. Where do you live? What do your days look like? Who are you spending time with? When you start giving your dream details, it goes from being a fuzzy or vague picture to something sharp, clear, and focused.

Right now, I want you to put down this book and pick up your notebook. Start writing and don't eliminate something just because you feel it is too farfetched. The more details, the better! Put on your 10-year-old hat and just let your imagination run wild.

If you are reading again, that means you have spelled out your dream life and thought about what would make you happy, spark joy, and inspire you. Still, you might be saying to yourself, how is writing down my dream life going to help me change the life I have right now? It starts with visualization.

How Does Visualizing Your Dream Help You Achieve It?

Your brain is amazing. It has the power to learn, to grow, and to make connections from your past knowledge and experiences to what you are learning right now. At every stage of your life, your brain is filing away information, memories, and emotions.

You smell pumpkin pie, and, in an instant, you are back in your mother's kitchen, fork in hand, ready to dig into that pie. Your brain takes the smells, sounds, and more from every experience, creating memories that you can access simply from one trigger or another, such as the smell of pie. Every part of your brain plays a role in shaping who you are, the memories you have, and the choices you make going forward, based on the beliefs and values built up throughout your lifetime.

Your brain also shapes your reality by judging whether a person is sincere, assigning motives and intentions to others, and then making decisions based on those assumptions. Since your brain is so powerful, it makes sense that visualizing what you want to achieve gives your brain something to create. Those creations can lead to an incredible life.

Your thoughts create your reality because your thoughts become the words you speak, and thus shape your beliefs. Our beliefs can be limiting, or they can propel us forward into the next phase of our lives. This is the process for changing our mindset and getting the results we want.

As you focus on visualizing, your brain starts looking for opportunities, some you might not have noticed in the past. What claims your focus often dictates what choices are laid out in front of you. Then you have the ability to make choices that take you closer to your dream life, or choices that drive you in the opposite direction.

The Law of Attraction defines your ability to attract what you focus on. Like attracts like, so whatever receives your energy and attention is what will be drawn back to you. Think about gravity. Even though you might not acknowledge it, gravity is at work in your life constantly. The Law of Attraction is also constantly at work in your life, whether you like it or not. So, if your life is not what you want, the first step is to change what you are focusing on. Visualizing is a means to do just that, while also shifting your mind away from the negative. If you focus on the positive, create a plan, and work toward your goals, then you will manifest whatever you can imagine. The Law of Attraction does not limit us; it simply gives back what we put into the universe.

As you visualize your goals and dreams, you teach your brain to recognize what resources are needed to achieve them. Your ability to see yourself achieving your dream makes it easier to promote positive thinking, which is key to staying on track to achieving your dreams.

Another aspect of visualization is the motivation it creates for you to act, taking steps to turn your vision into reality. When your vision of your life is so crystal clear in your mind, then you also can begin to see the steps necessary to achieve that vision.

When you feel that you are getting off track of where you want to be in life, then take the time to reset by focusing on your vision again. Spending time visualizing your dream life can motivate and inspire you to keep achieving your goals, thus turning that vision into your reality.

Remember, you can achieve what your mind believes. What you choose to think about will create your reality because our thoughts create the words that form our beliefs.

What Does Visualizing Involve?

Your vision is not some future state that you hope will happen. Instead, it needs to be treated as if everything in your vision already exists. Act as if you have already reached your dream. When you treat your vision as fact, then your brain and subconscious work to create that reality for you. Naturally, opportunities begin to stand out, and as you take advantage of them, it moves you closer to your dream life.

When you visualize something, your body is creating pathways and memories of how to do that action, even if you have never performed it before. The more time you spend visualizing your dream life, the better you get at perfecting the mental and physical aspects of your vision. It is like focusing energy, such as light, through a magnifying glass. This focused energy has a more powerful impact than light that is dispersed.

One of the best ways to visualize is to focus on your senses. What do you smell? What do you feel under your feet or when you reach out with your fingers? What do you see? What do you hear? The point is that when you are immersed in your vision, it feels real. When you truly desire something, then it becomes easier for you to focus your attention on it. The Law of Attraction can now come into play, thus allowing you to manifest your dreams.

Additionally, regularly visualizing your dream life will help you to start living as if you are already there. You begin to act differently, and that naturally allows you to find the opportunities that will draw you ever closer to what you have visualized.

Here are a few areas where you can put your focus as you visualize your future. Remember, the goal is to immerse yourself and embrace the vision with all your senses.

Romance: Do you have a partner right now? Is the relationship everything you hoped for? If not, what needs to happen? On the other hand, if you don't have a partner, do you want one? What does it feel like to have that special person in your life, to be in each other's company as you enjoy life together? What is it like to perform simple tasks together, like cooking dinner or going to a concert?

Travel: Do you want to travel? What is your dream destination? How does it feel to be there? How does it feel to hike in Patagonia, for instance?

Business: How does it feel to be a business owner, making decisions that help it to thrive? What type of freedom will owning a business give you in terms of your time and your finances?

Now list what you want to achieve. What does it feel like? How has it changed your life? How does it feel to have obtained it?

By thinking about these areas of life and focusing on what you want, and not limiting yourself in any way, you can craft a vision of your dream life that feels so real you could reach out and touch it!

How Can You Choose What to Include in Your Vision?

When it comes to visualizing your dream life, the most important thing to remember is to make it as realistic as possible. Include all the details that make it come to life in your mind. It might be tempting to edit your dream because you are focused on avoiding the impossible. This dream is about the second half of your life, and there are no limits!

Of course, your experiences to date have likely made it pretty clear what you don't want in your dream life. In fact, your life experiences might even help to clarify your dream even more. For instance, have you struggled with money in the past? Perhaps your dream life involves greater financial security, including money in your retirement or savings and the ability to pay down your bills.

If so, visualizing your dream should involve being detailed about what financial security looks like to you. After all, the Joneses might prefer to have three vacations a year and a new car in the driveway every other year, but your idea of financial security might be more focused on having a paid-off home and more flexibility to pursue opportunities without worrying about the financial payoff.

The point is that I want you to make it as realistic as possible. Do not be vague in describing your dream, and don't leave any details out. The beauty of visualization is that you can edit as your dream changes or details become clearer. The main thing to remember is that you have to spend time visualizing your dream life every day. I recommend doing so for a few minutes every morning. That will get your mind and thoughts focused on what you want to achieve, which can help you to avoid distractions.

The challenge you face is being disciplined enough to stick with visualizing daily, and then actively working in line with those thoughts to achieve your dreams and goals.

With that in mind, let's create a daily routine that allows you to give priority to your dreams throughout the day. These are tools you can use individually or in the pairing you choose:

Morning ritual – Take a few minutes every morning to visualize your dream life. Remember to make sure to include plenty of detail. Make it real. This focuses your thoughts for the day. Some individuals opt to do this when they first wake up, before they even get out of bed.

Evening ritual – Take a few minutes at the end of your day to visualize your dream life again. Put all those details into place. Make sure that you are relaxed so you can give this exercise your full attention.

Dream board – Your dream board is a physical representation of what you are visualizing on a daily basis. Make sure to include pictures, words, and other representations of your dreams. Regularly look at it throughout the day.

Video playlist – There are plenty of encouraging and motivating videos and podcasts out there that can provide you with a boost. Feed your mind thoughts and information that will encourage you to keep pursuing your dreams.

Dinner from your dream – What is your dream dinner? We all have one, and that could actually help you to figure out what else you want to include in your dream life. Your dream dinner could inspire a trip to another part of the world, like Greece. Remember that nothing is impossible, unless you decide it is.

Each of these aspects of visualization should be a regular part of your day. Spend time throughout the day looking at your dream board or adding to it. The goal is to keep your dreams front and center so that your thoughts and mind are constantly focused on them. However, distractions are everywhere, and once you are distracted, you can stop working toward your goals for the second half of your life. So how can you avoid getting distracted?

How to Avoid Getting Distracted from Your Vision

The world is designed to distract us from what we want to achieve. Every aspect of our day is filled with opportunities to get distracted away from our dreams and goals. Social media is just one aspect; the phone, which is likely sitting right by you as you read this, is another.

To avoid getting distracted by these things, pay attention to your compass. In the *Pirates of the Caribbean*, the compass was his heart, and it took the hero where he ultimately wanted to go. With visualizing, you focus on where you want to go, attracting what you need to get there. Allow your compass to lead you in the right direction.

The point of visualizing is not just about creating a beautiful picture in your mind. It involves becoming laser focused on what you want to achieve in your life, and then attracting the opportunities and resources necessary to bring it into reality.

Right now, I want you to list what you want to achieve. Remember, we are focused on details, to make it crystal clear in your mind.

- What does it feel like?
- Does it feel like you expected it to?
- Does it feel like the right fit or more like a shirt that is too tight across the shoulders?
- How will your life change when you achieve your dream?
- How does it feel to have obtained your dream?

Your dream life should expand and energize you. When you focus on these aspects of achieving your dream life, then you gain even more incentive to manifest it. Now that you have a clear vision of your dream life and are focused on that vision, let's talk about what it means to go where your vision is.

Chapter 5

You Go Where Your Vision Is

"The longest part of any journey is the delay from creating the idea to taking action."
– Steven Kanarian

Your vision is imperative to define your dream for the second half of your life. Your vision acts as your image of the destination, drawing you closer to your destination like a visual GPS route map. Explorers sailed across the Atlantic Ocean, imagining new lands and natural resources. This vision kept them focused during the challenges of their journeys. They were driven by the image of new lands, minerals and riches. See yourself having completed your journey and living the ideal second half of your life when you are imagining your vision. Feel the emotion of accomplishment and the satisfaction of having reached your goal. Let's dive into what your vision is, and how it can be the tool to keep you focused on creating the future you have always dreamed of building.

Your Vision: What Is Your Goal?

When defining your vision, you must see it in terms of your goals and how achieving them will impact your life. As we discussed in Chapter 4, you need to define what you want your life to look like clearly. Dreaming big is an important part of the process. Do not be quick to dismiss one part of your dream because it isn't realistic.

Once you have a clear vision of the life you want to live, it is time to start breaking that dream into goals. Each goal can be a small step, but it needs to be a step that moves you closer to achieving your dreams. Right now, let's set a few goals for Vinny, who wants to have a fishing guide business in the second half of his life.

Vinny has been an avid fisherman his entire life. He lives to fish and spends all his vacations exploring the rivers and lakes of Canada. He fishes and smokes his catch with flavors and woodchips. Vinny also makes and sells custom fishing rods, which are high quality and sold for hundreds of dollars. He puts his personal signature on each rod he makes.

Vinny plans for the day when he can retire and fish as a professional guide in upstate New York and Canada. Vinny told me he builds his business each year, with guide work. He plans to buy a camp to base his guide business and invest in high-quality canoes. Vinny's goals are listed in order of how he needs to achieve them to build his dream life.

When our vision comes to life through the process of completing our goals, we experience an incredible reward. How can you outline your goals and create meaningful steps to achieve your vision?

Take a few minutes and list the goals you would like to achieve in the second half of your life. Write what comes to your mind, and do not judge your choices. Be sure to put them in an order that makes sense for achieving them. We will revisit them later in this chapter.

Get Realistic and Set Timeframes

Let's look back at Vinny for a moment. He knew what his vision was and what he hoped to achieve, but without a clear path, it was unlikely that his vision would ever have come to fruition. Vinny complemented his vision with steps of action, bringing him closer to his goal of having a fishing guide retirement business. Many of our dreams can end up unfulfilled if we don't define the path to achieve them, and follow that path.

Plenty of people dream about what they would do with lottery winnings, but the only people who turn those dreams into reality are the ones who take action and buy a lottery ticket. I want you to start acting on your vision, step by step, instead of just imagining it and hoping it will occur someday. Ask yourself, "What can I do today to move the needle a degree or two towards my goal?"

So, how do you determine the best course of action to achieve your vision? You need to outline a path with specific goals and timeframes. Over the years, I have noticed that a deadline gets me moving more than a vague "someday." I often have to be against a deadline to get things done. This is an inherent side effect of being a paramedic for thirty years. We deal with emergencies in short timelines.

Another benefit of deadlines is that they can become a tool to measure our progress. What have we accomplished so far? Have we made enough progress to move on to another phase of our vision, or is there still work that needs to be done? How can you create deadlines that keep you moving toward your goal? I get a lot done before I leave for a trip. There is something about going to the airport that creates urgency for me. How can you create a sense of urgency to finish your work?

Goals with timeframes allow us to see where we might be falling short but also where we are finding success. Success is a great motivator to keep us on the path, even when we face minor setbacks.

When you map out the goals and timeline for achieving your vision, be realistic. I love people who enthusiastically start tackling the list, saying things like, "I'll have this done in a month or two." The problem is that the enthusiasm starts to wane when the list of goals to be finished is longer than the list of goals completed.

Success comes from doing tasks each day and gaining momentum with a system that generates results.

Being realistic can help you focus on the progress you have made so far without beating yourself up about the lengthy list of things still to do. Timelines help you stay focused, and finished goals demonstrate progress. Both can contribute to keeping you motivated. Be gentle on yourself if you miss a deadline or are work-focused for a while. You can get back on the path and move forward with action steps.

I have found that I fall into a fog of trying to do too many things simultaneously. I now create a visual list of things I want to achieve with colored paper notes. I prioritize the projects and focus on one thing until it is done. I had to say no to many things and spend some Saturday mornings working to complete this book. I started progressing when I was focused on completing the book and engaged an accountability partner to work with me. Writing a book by yourself is a daunting task. I am available to help guide you if you want to write a book or memoir. I can help you start by sharing the experience I gained developing the structure and outline.

My memoir is *The Downwind Walk: A USAR Paramedic's Experiences on September 11, 2001.* It is available on Amazon Books. I can be reached at Steve.2ndhalfoflife@outlook.com for coaching and help writing your memoir.

As your life begins to align with your vision, you might need to add more goals because areas of your vision become sharper in your mind. After all, with a clearer vision, some previous goals are no longer applicable.

Every journey is full of twists and turns, so do not be surprised if you also must adjust throughout this journey. The most important thing is to get started!

What Are the First Steps?

The first steps for setting goals to achieve a vision often start with research. After all, you don't know what you don't know.

Your vision starts with imagining the dream; how it looks, sounds and feels, and how it expands you. You should create your vision like an artist creates a painting. It should be clear, vibrant, and have details. You want your vision to be clear, like a Rembrandt painting, and not vague, like abstract art. I want to go to the Galapagos Islands one day. I envision the smell of the air, and the feel of the sand on my feet. I also think of the interesting animals I might see, and what it would be like to SCUBA dive in the ocean. Living, breathing and imagining your dream through the senses brings it to life.

For example, if your vision is to travel the world and explore various cultures, the first steps might include picking your first destination and places to stay, as well as making a list of activities to enjoy once you arrive. You can copy photos of your destination and read blogs about it. You can next make a physical dream board or create one online using a file organizing system like Evernote. Taking these steps will help your dream vision come to life.

Taking those first steps also might reveal changes you have to make in order to be successful. Leaving your comfort zone can be challenging, especially if your future success is still a work in progress. The fear of the unknown can be an obstacle that stops us from acting to achieve our goals.

Look at your goals. Are you dealing with a fear that is stopping you from acting? How can you change and address that fear successfully? Those changes might become sub-goals under your larger list of goals meant to achieve your vision.

The changes you are making might not initially make your vision materialize, but what they will do is help you become the person who can turn your vision into a reality. Personal growth naturally seems to occur as we focus on achieving our goals and manifesting our visions to live amazing lives.

When you are open to change, you might find that your vision manifests even faster. Open minds and open hearts tend to draw opportunities, and when we act on those opportunities, big things start to happen.

Are You Measuring Your Progress?

Do you remember doing experiments in your science class during elementary school? A key part of those experiments was writing down your results. You had to have a regular time to measure the growth of your plants, for example, and then put that measurement in your chart. As the weeks went by, you could see how much your plant was growing, not just by looking at it but by the data you collected.

When achieving your vision and bringing it to life, you need to stay motivated. Most of your dreams and goals won't be achieved in a few days or a week. They will require time and effort, so you need ways to stay motivated. One way is to measure your progress. Earlier in this chapter, I had you write your goals down in order. The idea is to check off those goals as you achieve them. That can be a great motivator.

Another way to measure your success is by milestones. You can define milestones that celebrate small successes during your dream-building journey. I set milestones for this book to reward myself and measure my success. When I finished the book, I promised myself I would go SCUBA diving in the Cayman Islands. Effectively using milestones can help you stay motivated during your dream-building process. What is the dream you would like to build for the second half of your life?

Your dream life is a vision on the wall or in your journal, but as you achieve goals, that vision becomes part of your reality. It might be in bits and pieces, but it will happen. You must believe, and be willing to put in the effort.

I have always been excited to try new things. Our quality of life improves dramatically when we are willing to step outside of the comfort zone we created. It isn't always easy, but once we do, we will probably kick ourselves and ask why we didn't do it sooner.

I have always found that my attitude improves when I am working towards a goal. I have also found, through experience, that the act of doing something uncomfortable is always easier than anticipating and considering potential problems.

Your vision is meant to become a part of your life. You must reach out to achieve it and be willing to make changes. Those changes might be hard initially, but they can also open the door to greater opportunities.

I want you to measure your progress to see how far you have come and the number of opportunities that have presented themselves. Are you building connections with those individuals who can give you the benefit of their experience or who can point you in the right direction to achieve specific goals?

At this juncture, measuring progress also assists you in defining where you are right now and where you want to be. Your goals are meant to bridge the distance between the two so, as you complete various goals on your list, you can visualize your bridge coming to life. In the beginning, early goals might be preparation for the bridge supports to fall into place.

Later goals might be the actual supports, followed by the bracing and, finally, the boards of the bridge itself. What is neat about a bridge from where you are to where you want to be is that when you start making changes, you are already shortening that gap and moving closer to your destination.

This chapter is about imagining your dream vision, setting meaningful goals, putting them in an actionable timeline, and measuring your progress. Every part of this chapter is focused on action. Nothing will ever come into place without your willingness to act. Even in the face of setbacks—and you will have them—the only way to move forward is by defining a course of action and then being disciplined enough to follow that path.

Up to this point, your vision has likely been in your mind, and your journal is full of lists and goals. But your vision can be difficult to pin down if it isn't tangibly brought into your reality, at least in the earliest stages. That is why I recommend creating a vision board. The vision board will bring your vision into your space and provide a tangible reference to help you refocus on your dream when you get distracted.

Vision boards are also great because, as you get a clearer picture of what you want to achieve, you can edit them to reflect better the life you want to lead.

In the 1980s, I dreamed of going to Australia. I envisioned snorkeling in the Great Barrier Reef and seeing Ayers Rock. I dreamed of this for several years, all the while delaying the trip. I read stories of explorers who went to Australia, and I learned about the country. My friend JoAnn took me to dinner at the World Trade Center during the Windows on the Worlds, when they had an Australia Week feature menu. Going to dinner at Windows on the World helped make the dream feel more real.

I did not want to go alone. I eventually learned that my friend Bill's brother Glen was interested in going and could take a month off. We agreed to travel together, and I soon headed to the travel agent's office. I will never forget it. Booking the trip took about an hour, and we were off on our journey to Australia to visit Melbourne, Perth, Sydney, and the Great Barrier Reef. I will never forget how quickly the booking process was over once we decided to go. Years of anticipation and planning resulted in this trip. Even though the flight to Sydney is sixteen hours from Los Angeles, taking action was the longest part of the journey. Glen and I had a great time in Australia, and we made friends with travelers there for years.

It is important to create your dream and chart the path to building your second half of life, but it is also important to take action and start the journey. You may have to revise your plan and vision, but that is all part of a successful journey. Let's explore what a vision board is and how you can create one for yourself.

Chapter 6

Building Your Vision Board

"If you can conceive it and believe it, you can achieve it."
– W. Clement Stone

As people, most of us are very visual. We are inspired by what we see around us, be it the birds, the night sky, or even just the beautiful view from our front porch. Having lived and worked in one of the biggest cities in the world, I know that the skyline can take your breath away.

How does this relate to fulfilling our dreams? When we keep a dream in our heads, it tends to stay there. We don't make progress. The tangible aspects of our dreams can get fuzzy or disappear altogether. One of the ways I encourage my clients to help give their dreams a tangible quality is through a vision board. Let's talk about what they are and how they can be used effectively to get you moving toward that dream life in your second half.

Why Is a Vision Board Important?

Your vision board is very similar to the collages we used to make in school as part of a history or art project. Yet, for a vision board, each image you choose to include represents your dreams. You can choose images that inspire you or images that help motivate you to act, especially when things get difficult.

The importance of a vision board is that it gives you a physical manifestation of your dreams, something that you can focus on to help you self-reflect on how your current choices are shaping the future you want for yourself. Are you making choices and taking steps that move you closer to achieving your dreams or sending you in the opposite direction?

Vision boards assist you in imagining the future, giving it the detail and clarity that increases your positive emotional response and optimism regarding your ability to achieve these dreams. Positive emotions and thoughts make it easier for you to find opportunities you might have otherwise missed.

While there is no concrete research on the benefits of vision boards, there is much antidotal evidence to support their use in achieving goals and dreams. Vision boards are not magic, but they can help you gain clarity and focus about what you want to manifest in your life.

Being able to see my future in color on my vision board gives me a jolt of positivity, especially when I struggle with different setbacks or other challenges. Focusing on the visual images can remind you that the current situation is only temporary. Too often, we get caught up in the short term and project these setbacks onto our long-term dreams and goals, believing they are impossible to achieve. That isn't the case. Anything is possible, but we have to act to achieve it.

How Do You Build Your Vision Board?

First, how you create your visual representation of your dreams and goals is up to you. Some individuals opt to use magazine images or pictures, colors, and textures to craft their vision boards. Others include song lyrics, meaningful quotes, or other things that represent their goals, desires, and dreams. The point of this section isn't to give you tips on how to be crafty, but on how to choose the right areas to represent to make your vision board effective for you. Also, you want your vision board to reflect where you are in your journey. I like to post photos from magazines or a brochure for my next cruise to Italy and Greece. Naturally, that means talking about how your vision board can change as you move through your life and achieve your goals, which we will discuss later in this chapter.

The truth is that what motivates me is not going to motivate you. Our values, beliefs, and goals shape and motivate us to achieve our dreams. So, before you grab the scissors, corkboard, and pins, let's start by getting to the heart of who you are and the seed of your motivation.

What Are Your Values?

You can set a lot of goals, creating a list a mile long. But those goals will stay on paper unless you can get excited about achieving them. The best motivation is when our goals align with our values. When you achieve a goal that aligns with your values, there is greater satisfaction and accomplishment.

To figure out your values, ask yourself:

- What really matters to me?
- What gives meaning to my life?
- What type of person do I want to be?
- Who do I need to help me move forward?
- What type of support is essential to me (emotional, spiritual, mental, accountability, etc.)?
- How do I want to spend my time?

These questions can give you the ability to zero in on your values and how well your goals and dreams align with them. Once you understand your values more fully, then you can easily take on the challenge of choosing goals that align with them. Suddenly, you are motivated to act and achieve your goals because they align with who you are and the person you want to be in this world. I have pictures on my dream board that remind me of the family life I want to have, the ocean, scuba diving, travel, and my health.

As you pursue your goals, remind yourself of what you want and why you want it. Are there past experiences that play a role in your dreams and goals? Some individuals focus on having greater financial security because of what they experienced in childhood, and their goals for shaping their lives have this constant thread of financial security and stability running through them. By understanding why your goals and dreams are important, you can be motivated to achieve them. As a coach, I help you dive into your values and motivations, helping you to give voice to these things that you might not have been clear about in the past. The clearer your vision is, the closer you are to realizing your dreams.

Set priorities.

Up to this point, I have spent a lot of time trying to get you to abandon limiting thoughts and a mindset that keeps you from taking risks, exploring your dreams, and creating your amazing second half. Now, I need you to take all your dreams and bring a touch of realism into the mix. That means setting timeframes, giving priority to some goals so that you can see a greater level of progress.

Your vision board needs to reflect your priorities, or it will simply end up being a collection of your goals and dreams. There is no action plan. So, I want you to craft your vision board by dividing it into multiple areas based on timeframes. What progress can you reasonably make in one year, five years, or even ten years? Put your goals into groups, allowing you to prioritize the ones that can be completed quickly to keep you motivated to finish long-term ones.

Additionally, determine what needs to be done first and what needs your time and attention. When you have multiple dreams, it is hard to make any progress on any of them if you get so scattered that nothing gets completed. By putting a priority list in place, you can stay focused and direct your efforts where you can get the most accomplished.

Your vision board can be set up to reflect your priorities. Those are the things that dominate your vision board, either at the top, center, or just a majority of the board overall. You can structure your vision board in any way that you like, but please remember that it needs to be there to give you motivation, remind you of what you want to achieve, and also help you to stay focused and avoid distractions. Now, let's shift our focus to the main areas of your life that can be included on your vision board.

What Are Some of the Essential Things to Include?

There are many dreams that you can include on your vision board, but for now, I want you to focus on a few key areas. By doing so, you can stay disciplined and focused on these areas, which can help you to make more progress. You can define your dreams in these areas with plenty of detail on your vision board. These main areas are the following:

- Financial
- Relationships
- Health
- Dream Home
- Travel/Adventures
- Career

As you stop to work on each of these areas of your vision board, find items that make it clear to you what your goals are and when you want to see them finished. That can help to trigger a sense of urgency, especially when you deal with setbacks that can leave you feeling frustrated and discouraged.

While there are no set rules for how your vision board will look, the goal is to give you a place to reflect and refocus so that you can achieve your dreams. Now, while I might have a focus on several areas of my life at once, others would tend to focus on one single idea. You might opt to embrace every aspect of your long-term future, or simply a small chunk of it that you can achieve within a few short weeks or months. The only thing that every vision board should include is a clear picture of what you want in your life.

Gaining Clarity Through Your Vision Board

"The longest part of any journey is from the idea to taking action."
– Steven Kanarian

Transitioning to the next stage of your life involves knowing how you want that next stage to look and feel. Perhaps you don't have a lot of clarity about your future, just a few vague dreams. Throughout these first few chapters, you might have started to define them, but they aren't necessarily crystal clear. If that is the case, then your vision board could be just the tool you are looking for to find that clarity of purpose and thought.

Creating your vision board isn't going to happen in one afternoon or a few hours. Instead, take the time to determine what you want to include. If you have a clue about one area of your life, then focus on clarifying your vision in just that area. Don't put added stress on yourself to move beyond that area. What is interesting is that as you work on one area of your life, clarity regarding other areas begins to make itself apparent.

The best part of your vision board is that it can be refined as you fulfill your goals and your dreams morph into something else. You can be living your dream life but still find areas where you want to achieve something else or even refine your purpose.

You should use your vision board as a reminder of what your ideal life will look like. See the desired life, feel it, and hear the sounds that go with the dream. What will it feel like to walk the streets of Italy with the cobblestones under your feet. What smells will be in the air from the restaurants you pass?

A TV commercial is a very intentionally crafted visual message to appeal to the things you desire in life, whether the desired goal you have is to be healthy, to be adventurous, to travel, or to win the adoration of friends. TV commercials appeal to viewers so companies can sell them their products. Visualization is a very effective method of selling products.

As you find clarity, your intention becomes apparent. Once you have an intention, the ideas on how to bring that intention to life start to flood into place. Your vision board helps you to set your intentions, which then gives you the ability to define the actions that will bring them to fruition.

Can Your Vision Board Ever Change?

The interesting thing about vision boards is that they are not fixed. You can always make changes to reflect who you are and what you want to accomplish throughout your life's journey. When you analyze your vision board, you can see how much it reveals about who you are and what you want to get out of your life.

That means, as your intentions and priorities change, your vision board should change too. Keep in mind that your goals will develop, and new things will come into your life, which can mean you need to reassess your action plan for your life. Of course, your vision board should be revised to reflect what is happening in your life. After all, it can't keep you focused if it doesn't reflect where you are right now and the direction you want to go.

How can you effectively edit your vision board? You can always take parts of your vision board away, add new things, or even remove those goals that are outdated or have been achieved. This is a working document to refine whenever you find it necessary to do so. Filter out aspects of your vision board that feel less important or are no longer relevant, so your board remains a source of inspiration and motivation.

At this point, you might be wondering why I spent this time focusing on vision boards in such detail. Part of it is about manifesting what you want in your life. You achieve what you focus on, and what grabs your attention and holds on to it.

Vision boards can be a way to stay on track when life throws things your way that could end up taking you wildly off course. It can help you to track your daily tasks and guide you toward achieving everything on your board. Instead of forgetting your goals because life got busy, you keep them directly in your focus through your vision board. Learning and then mastering the art of discipline and focus are powerful tools, because they can assist you in managing your mindset effectively. Creating a vision board helps you keep your concentration on your target, which is achieving your dream life in the second half.

In the 1980s, I became obsessed with going to Australia. This desire was probably due to the Australian advertisements to "Come visit the land down under." I placed pictures from the Australian tour guide in my apartment. I was introduced to a visiting emergency medical technician from Australia. A friend took me to the Windows on the World restaurant during Australian Week. I wanted to go but did not have a person to travel with. The final piece of the picture was in place once I found a person to travel with, and I made the reservations: one month of travel to four cities in Australia. A total of twelve flights were booked. I was amazed how it only took an hour to book the trip once the decision was made to take action. I traveled with Glenn to Australia and it was the journey of a lifetime. We went to Sydney, Melbourne, Perth, and the Great Barrier Reef. We enjoyed the country and made friends from other countries. I snorkeled in the Great Barrier Reef. The whole experience started with a vision, the support of friends helping me toward that goal of traveling to Australia, and the decision to take action.

The trip now seems easy. Looking back at the decision to go, I remember not feeling comfortable and dealing with objections in my mind. I made the trip with ease once the vision was complete, and my friends helped me make the vision feel real.

But life is never cut and dried, or I wouldn't have been called to people's homes at the worst moments of their lives when I was a paramedic. So, I know better than anyone how obstacles and the unexpected can throw off your plans and make you reassess your goals. With that in mind, I want to shift to one of my favorite areas of coaching, which is how you can overcome obstacles and challenges by identifying them early on and creating a game plan to deal with them if they do arise.

Chapter 7

Identifying Obstacles to Your Dream

Your vision board is full of your dreams and goals and serves as a constant reminder of what you can achieve with the right mindset and action plan. But life has a funny way of throwing up challenges, sending curveballs your way. I am from the East Coast, where road construction is considered one of the seasons. When you set your GPS, you have a path to follow to get to your destination. It is the fastest route. But then construction happens and, suddenly, you are detoured. What was just going to be a two-hour trip has gotten significantly longer. Plus, as you deal with the detours, you might find yourself in unfamiliar territory, increasing the likelihood that you are going to get lost. It is a struggle to stay on course, and part of you is ready to simply give up and go home. But most of the time, we stick with it, despite the detours to our route, and end up reaching our destination, satisfied that we accomplished what we set out to do.

Life tends to do that with our dreams. We have come up with an action plan, the shortest route to achieving our dreams, and then bam! Road construction happens and we have to detour. Along the way, we keep encountering different options, choices about what turns to make, and how to keep ourselves on track even in unfamiliar territory.

You can easily see that these situations have what we would term as obstacles. An obstacle is a barrier, a blockade that stops us from moving forward. It can actively derail us from achieving our goals and dreams. The problem with obstacles is that you can view them as a stop sign, deciding that you can't go any further, or you can see them as a challenge to be overcome so that you can continue on the path to achieving your dreams.

This chapter is all about obstacles and how you can turn them from being dream enders to being solutions that can accelerate your journey to achieving your vision for your life.

Is It Really an Obstacle?

The definition of obstacle, according to Merriam-Webster dictionary[1], is "something that impedes progress or achievement." Other dictionaries define it as a "thing that blocks one's way or prevents or hinders progress." While you might immediately think of obstacles as being something that happens outside of your control, the truth is that you can be your own worst enemy, creating obstacles for yourself and derailing the path to your dreams. Obstacles really only stop us when we opt to let them. Think about all the different people you see in the news with inspiring stories about overcoming multiple obstacles, such as strokes, losing a limb, growing up in a dysfunctional household, dealing with trauma or abuse, and even incredible loss. They all had moments when the circumstances were so difficult that they had the option to simply quit. And yet, they didn't quit. They found a way to deal with the obstacles, even if it meant just muscling through the pain or getting necessary care for their mental health—but they didn't give up or quit.

---

[1] Obstacle Definition & Meaning - Merriam-Webster

Truthfully, there is no obstacle in the world that can stop you from achieving your dreams unless you give it the power to do so. We all have moments where the obstacles seem to pile on. While we can't control what happens to us, we have the ability to control how we handle what happens to us.

Will you decide that the dream is too big and quit?

Will you decide to push through the obstacle, even if it means taking a slight detour to achieve your dreams?

Every success in your life up to this point has come with obstacles that you have to overcome by creating the solutions necessary to achieve your goals. Obstacles can be limiting factors that hinder your progress, but if you see them as problems that need solutions, then you can find a way to get past the obstacles to achieve your dreams.

Define Your Obstacles

Right now, you might be facing some obstacles. They might even be stacked on top of each other, making you feel as if you are falling behind or simply not ready to achieve your dreams. The truth is, if you can name the obstacle, then you can find a way to deal with it. Right now, you have the opportunity to clearly define your obstacles and what challenges they might be creating. Then you can move toward a solution. Once you know what the problem is, you can find the resources to move toward a solution. Let's discuss a few common obstacles and how they can play a role in pushing you off the path to your dreams.

The Objections of Others

You might be surprised to realize that some of your greatest obstacles are the people who are constantly buzzing in your ear about what you are capable of achieving. These are the people who are not lifting you up, but instead are focused on bringing you down. Their negative talk can get into your head so much that you start to believe what they are saying. Their objections can grow to the point that they feed your self-doubt. You might also feel so overwhelmed by all the objections and problems they bring up, you decide to give up. Objections can create problems that don't really exist except in the minds of those who are raising them. Yet, you stop moving forward because of these invisible problems.

How can you overcome this obstacle?

Start by setting boundaries. Instead of talking endlessly about their objections, tell them you want to discuss something else. Be honest with yourself about your relationships. Are their reactions based on jealousy or envy because they see you as succeeding in areas where they have struggled? It might be time to reevaluate the relationship.

The most supportive relationships are ones where you both can be honest with each other, encourage each other, and brainstorm together about solutions. They should be in your corner, giving your realistic feedback but not dream-killing. If they are dream-killers, then it may be time to end the relationship altogether.

Additionally, be reasonable about their objections. Are they really likely to happen, or is it possible that those objections are only problematic in the minds of others? Once you recognize the real challenges from the unlikely ones, you can focus your energy and time on finding necessary solutions. Your dreams will stay intact, regardless of the objections of others.

Feeling of Self-Doubt

I have dealt with moments where I felt inadequate for the task in front of me, especially during my time as a paramedic. Despite all your training and knowledge, sometimes you simply can't help, and it can lead to self-doubt. Did you do everything possible? Was there a detail you missed that could have made a difference?

In our lives, we all have moments of self-doubt. The obstacle comes into play when we decide to let our self-doubt stop us from acting to achieve our dreams. The problem is that self-doubt is based on our own thoughts and feelings. When we don't trust ourselves to make good decisions, then we question every move and overanalyze it to the point that we might even be too paralyzed to make a decision at all.

Others around you can feed into your self-doubt, making you question your path or simply give up on achieving it. Their objections could be based on their concern for you, envy that you are going after your dreams, or fear that if you achieve your dreams, the relationship between you will change.

Overcoming mindset issues and negativity that can be paralyzing to your dreams is essential. We know ourselves pretty well and know the things that cause us to procrastinate. I suggest making a list of obstacles you think you will encounter and writing down potential solutions to that problem. The doubt surrounding not knowing what to do can cost you weeks and months in reaching your goals. I hired a business coach when starting my coaching business because I had never been down this road before. I have years of experience coaching people and guiding them to success, but I have never started my own business and wanted the winning recipe from the start.

I know the things I may encounter while starting a new project. I know for example that technological details sometimes delay my project. I have learned to look at YouTube videos, call a friend who is good in tech, or hire someone to do that part for me. You will benefit by listing the obstacles you may encounter and a course of action. If you find you have mindset and growth issues from past experiences, you may need a coach. I often work with clients who are deciding on a new career, finding a passion in retirement, or needing help in getting from the dream state to success. As your coach, I can help you identify and overcome obstacles to determine the path to success and clarify your dream vision. Email me at Steve.2ndhalfoflife@outlook.com if you would like to discuss the possibility of working together to ensure your success in the second half of life.

But fundamentally, overcoming self-doubt means trusting yourself, as well as being able to take risks to achieve your goals. That requires overcoming self-doubt and the habit of questioning your decisions constantly.

Clearly, to overcome self-doubt takes work on our part. We need to be disciplined about how we think and not allow that doubt to creep in. Be confident that the decisions you are making are the right ones for you. They might not fit everyone else's idea of the best path, but this is your journey, not theirs.

Taking time each day to listen to your inner voice can be the best way to help you overcome your self-doubt. And if something doesn't feel right, you don't need to stick with it. You can always make adjustments. Just because you made a decision to go one way doesn't mean that you can't course correct as necessary. Circumstances will change, so you need to be flexible.

The point of adapting and being flexible is that you adjust as circumstances shift. Those adjustments don't mean you made the wrong decision in the first place; it just means you have to shift to stay on course. To be honest, these types of adjustments remind me of sailing. As the wind changes, you might have to tighten up the sails or loosen them. But once you make those adjustments, you can stay on course and reach your destination. So instead of doubting yourself, focus on making the corrections necessary to keep yourself on course, and enjoy what you learn about yourself through this process.

Overcoming Negativity

We all have that one co-worker or friend who can find the problem in every solution. Their main job is to find problems you didn't even know existed and point them out to you. When you get excited and tell them about an opportunity, they will tell you why that opportunity isn't worth pursuing. Likely, after a discussion with these friends, you feel your energy drained, and you might even be wondering if you should move forward with your action plan.

How do you manage the negative energy coming from these individuals? The truth is that you are not going to change who they are, so you need to find a way to adjust. First, you need to set boundaries with those who are negative. It might mean walking away when conversations go negative and the discussion turns to how you shouldn't do that or can't accomplish those dreams. Be clear about what you are willing to tolerate.

Second, be honest that you won't engage in negative discussions that have no purpose. Once others see that your conversation is focused on uplifting and encouragement for others and their dreams, then you demonstrate for them a different type of energy.

No matter what, you don't need people tearing you down as you enter this second half. You want to spend time with the people who continue to build you up. As you focus on the second half, remember that you also need to be uplifting when it comes to the dreams of others. If you don't want them tearing down your dreams and goals, then you need to do the same. Give them encouragement, especially when challenges arise. I encourage you to do this with your children. Let them reach for their dreams and be supportive. You might be surprised how that can boomerang back as you continue on this journey of shaping your second half.

Counting the Costs

You have reached this stage of your life focused on counting the costs of everything. Decisions were likely made based on the available resources, the needs of your family, and your income. Perhaps you made sacrifices to ensure that your children went to college or had the things they needed to be successful in various areas of their lives.

The result is that you have reached the second half of your life with an eye on the budget. It can be so easy to edit our dreams to fit what is in our bank account. You have worked for decades, and you might not have the same drive to work 60+ hours that you had in your twenties and thirties.

So, when you look at your vision board, your mind naturally starts to edit, focusing on what you can get rid of to fit your pocketbook. You see money as a limiting factor and begin to act as if it is the end of all of your dreams. But opportunities have a way of growing and becoming apparent once you focus your mind and energy on finding them.

You are manifesting your dreams and bringing them to life. Don't let money become the limiting factor that keeps you stuck in a rut with a job or routine that doesn't feed your soul. You did that enough in the first half, and it left you feeling frustrated and overwhelmed. The second half is about finding ways to make your dreams come true.

There is going to be work, but you deserve to find joy in your second half. You might be saying, "That's all well and good, Steve. But how can you find cash when it simply isn't available?"

I tend to focus on getting creative. Money can stretch in a variety of ways. Manifesting the life you want will take time and effort, but with creativity, anything is possible. Your mind, being focused on your goals and dreams, can help you to find opportunities where you might not have seen them before, thus making financial options appear as well.

Don't let costs and financial decisions stop you from pursuing your dreams. You might need to start small, but each step will get you closer to achieving that dream life. With each obstacle you encounter, there are ways to get past them. Just don't let an obstacle be the reason you quit. This is your second half. Even if you are dealing with circumstances that are making it difficult to move forward, you still have time to make the right calls to achieve a winning second half.

Chapter 8

Support and Resources to Blast Those Obstacles

"I don't want to regret not becoming the person I know I could be, just because I'm scared to take the risks that I know I need to take."
– Topher Kearby

In Chapter 7, we focused on different obstacles and how you might address them. But obstacles are not just financial or the words of others. Circumstances, including the loss of a spouse, health issues, and other challenges, are going to pop up as you work to manifest your dream life in the second half.

While I can't list out every possible scenario that you might encounter, the truth is that you can have certain tools in your toolbox to assist you in managing when obstacles do arise. These tools are resources, meant to give you the ability to create an action plan to deal with your new circumstances, while not derailing you from achieving your goals. With that in mind, let's dive into some of these tools and the ways you can effectively utilize them.

What Is the Real Obstacle?

Obstacles present natural opportunities for us to learn and grow. Along with a willingness to learn, you need to have a mindset that thrives on adversity and is resilient. Building resiliency comes from recognizing obstacles and then creating a plan to work through them. It is not easy to be resilient, especially when you are faced with difficult circumstances. As a paramedic, I saw people deal with tragic losses. They had to find a way to keep moving forward, despite what they were dealing with emotionally and mentally.

For you, identifying the obstacles is the first step. Once you define a problem, finding the solution is possible. Notice that I didn't say finding the solution was going to be easy. It isn't always a piece of cake. In fact, some days, the solution might be the choice between two bad options. You are just trying to figure out which one is less awful.

Other days, the solutions will end up being two opportunities. The question is, which one is the right one for you? I am always amazed at how difficult it can be to choose an opportunity, simply because you don't always know if it is ultimately going to take you down the right path. Weighing opportunities often comes down to which one aligns more closely with the vision board, with that ideal dream life you want to manifest.

Obstacles can be a way to uncover opportunities, but they can also show you where you have a block and assist you in creating changes that move the block out of the way. For example, take family members that discourage you from pursuing your dreams. They might focus on your age, your financial situation, or even your dreams themselves. The point is that the obstacle they present is the seeds of doubt they sow within you. How can you get rid of that block? It might involve setting boundaries about what you will discuss and what you won't. I have gotten up and walked away plenty of times, simply because it isn't worth it to bring that level of negativity into my life. You have to be willing to make the same decision. After all, feedback about ways to make your dreams come true is one thing, but when someone constantly picks at your dreams, trying to discourage you from pursuing them, then that is a relationship you need to consider changing.

Perhaps you don't have that as an obstacle, but you are struggling with having the financial resources to make your dreams come true. If you want to own a business, you might be wondering how you can bring that business to life without capital. For you, the solution is finding ways to build contacts and find capital, either through loans or investors. You are taking a risk to achieve your dreams. Without risk, there is no reward.

The obstacle of losing a spouse or partner can be a huge setback, in large part because of the role they played in supporting you throughout the pursuit of your dreams. Now you are dealing with the realities of life without them, and it can drain your motivation to move forward.

Analyzing your circumstances involves identifying what might be holding you back or keeping you from moving forward. Obstacles can also happen when you are working down a path and find yourself stuck, unable to make any further progress. The point is that you can't find the solution or begin to make progress unless you know what is holding you back in the first place. Then you need to be willing to make a change, even if the change itself is hard. Doing a hard thing to make progress can often be the only course open to you, but it is worth the effort.

Eliminate Overthinking

When you face an obstacle, it can become your whole focus. Your mind just continues to focus inward as you try to find the best solution. However, as you mull over that situation, your emotional response becomes focused on how unhappy you are or how stressed and frustrating the situation is. A solution isn't forthcoming, but your heightened emotions make it less likely that you can see your circumstances clearly. The result is that you just lose motivation and have an increase in negative thinking.

But it isn't easy to stop overthinking, especially if the circumstances can have a profound impact on your ability to achieve your dreams. With that in mind, let's talk about some practical ways to avoid overthinking or to break the cycle of overthinking once it starts.

Distract yourself by finding something fun to do that diverts your attention away from the obstacles or problems you are facing. Sometimes, just changing your physical surroundings by going for a walk can get your mind off that problem for a while. Plus, you might be surprised at how quickly a solution can appear once your mind isn't focused on the obstacle.

Switch your thoughts by focusing on something that brings you joy instead of stress. You might even need to make a conscious decision to stop thinking about the problem, even telling yourself to stop. It isn't easy, but it is definitely worth the effort.

Write it out in your journal. It can allow you to get your thoughts organized and help you to identify the real concerns.

Talk with a friend about your concerns. Let them give their perspective. It might help you to identify the potential solutions, or at least get a clearer idea of what your concerns are and what you need to actually address immediately to reduce your stress.

Give yourself time to just vent and overthink the situation. But set a time limit. Don't allow yourself to dwell unnecessarily beyond that limit. It can let you explore your emotions without judgment.

The truth is that negative thought patterns can happen, but you don't want them to become obsessive. It doesn't help the situation and can even make it more difficult for you to find solutions or even make rational decisions about the direction you need to take in the future.

What You Can Solve Versus What You Have to Let Go

The truth is that some obstacles are simply going to exist without a solution bubbling up to the surface. You simply have to find a way to be comfortable with the circumstances and be at peace with them. That might mean finding a small step you can take to continue moving yourself toward your goals and not letting the obstacles completely overwhelm you.

You need to remember that taking action, however small, can be the ticket to getting unstuck and moving forward. Solutions that are not always apparent can often appear when we start focusing on taking small steps forward. The wisdom to know when you can solve a problem and when you just have to let it go is often what you need when faced with an obstacle.

Don't spend a lot of time focusing on what you can change; stay focused on what you can do. Remember your strengths and allow them to come to the surface. There will be things you simply can't change, but dwelling on that doesn't do anything but increase your stress level.

When coaching clients, I help them to shift their focus toward what they can do and give them strategies to keep from dwelling on the negative or the things they can't alter about their circumstances. Building your resilience can help you to harness your inner strength and thus rebound from the setbacks or challenges that come your way.

Being resilient does not mean your problems just go away with the snap of your fingers. Instead, it gives you the ability to see beyond the current circumstances and find joy in your life. Resiliency also helps you to manage your stress more effectively as you adapt to the difficult situations that can present themselves.

Perhaps you might be struggling with your resilience, particularly in the light of your current circumstances. Here are a few ways that your resilience can grow:

- Get connected with strong, positive relationships that provide support, guidance, and acceptance.

- Establish connections by volunteering or spending time with your faith community.

- Make every day meaningful by doing something that gives you a sense of accomplishment, even if it is just a small task that moves you toward your goals.

- Reflect on past experiences where you coped with challenges. You can identify positive and negative behavior patterns, then use that information to guide your future decisions as you deal with your current challenges.

- Take care of yourself by participating in activities that bring you joy and peace.

- Get plenty of sleep and be sure to maintain your healthy eating habits.

- Practice forms of stress management, even if it is as simple as going for a walk, deep breathing, guided imagery, or even meditation.

- Remain hopeful but be proactive. You don't want to ignore your problems; create an action plan. Even after you resolve the problem, you still need time to recover. Know that your situation will improve if you work at it.

Beyond building your resiliency, self-care is also important. To prepare to take on the challenges that you face as you work toward your dreams, you have to take care of yourself physically. You won't achieve your goals if you are running around with zero energy. Of course, the normal things apply here, such as adequate sleep, good nutrition, and making time for exercise.

Self-care goes beyond the physical and extends to your emotional needs as well. After all, if you aren't taking care of your emotional needs, you can end up feeling burned out, and that can negatively impact your ability to achieve your dreams. How can you effectively care for your emotional needs?

Make time for your hobbies and activities that bring you joy, since this can be rejuvenating. Incorporate these activities into your daily life, not making them something that happens just once in a while. Practice self-compassion as well. You are not always going to get everything right on the first try. When you fall down, don't see that as a sign that your dreams are too far out of reach. Failure is just a chance for you to learn and grow. Reaching your dreams will never be a straight path forward. In fact, most of the time, it will be full of twists and turns. Obstacles are just part of that process, and you will not always solve them right away. Instead, focus on what is in your power to change right now, and let what you can't change go.

Learn to Manage Your Stress

When things are going smoothly, we all enjoy the lack of stress. You can't help but think, this is the best life! It will always be this amazing. The truth is that life doesn't work like that. Instead, the good times are great, but eventually the good times will be replaced with struggles and sorrows. But you know what? Eventually, those struggles and sorrows will be replaced by good times. Everything moves in and out of your life in turns.

With that in mind, the only thing you can control is how you respond to these movements of the good and the bad times. You control your stress level. If you find that you don't deal with your stress but tend to ignore it, then you will find that unhealthy habits related to your stress will develop. Finding healthy ways to cope with your stress is key to long-term happiness and success.

When you are pursuing your dreams, you will find that success often hinges on your ability to manage difficult situations and manage your stress level. The more stressed you are, the harder it can be to find the solution to a problem or manage your relationships in a positive way.

As part of my coaching, I focus on helping you to identify your stress triggers and create strategies to manage your stress more effectively. To manage our stress and the challenges that life throws at us, we need to not only understand our reactions and create healthy habits, but we also must build a support system that can give us the necessary tools to be successful. Let's dive into what a support system can look like and how it can be an essential part of achieving the vision for your life that you laid out on your vision board.

Your "Go-to" Resource List for Dealing with Obstacles

A delay due to uncertainty can cost you days or weeks in a project. I remember writing my book, *The Downwind Walk: A Paramedics Experiences on September 11, 2001.* I would have a problem relating to a scene from September 11th and take a few weeks to chew on the issue. "How do I represent this incident? Is this incident too much for public reading?"

You can keep your project in the flow state by having a list of resources and people to go to when you have a question.

I am always amazed how talking to another person about an issue will bring about conversation and a solution. Often, the solution comes from within me and is brought out through collaboration.

The problems you anticipate during the pursuit of your dream are usually known to you. You can keep your progress on track by making a resource list and planning to handle the unknown.

<u>Example of resource sheet:</u>

Format:

"For problems with:"

- *"I will take this step to alleviate the problem:"*

Example:

If I run into a problem publishing my blog:

- I will prepare by reading a book on making a WordPress Blog.
- I will take an online mini course.
- I will look on YouTube.
- I will look at WordPress videos.
- I will consult my techie wizard friend Brian.
- I will look online for a tech to hire for the role.

Setting up my business:

- I will reach out to my local business development agency.
- I will reach out to a mentor in the business world.
- I will consult a lawyer.
- I will discuss the issue with a mentor or my coach.

For problems with focus and mindset:

- I will reach out to Steven Kanarian, my coach.

For planning to travel in my motorhome in the USA:

- I will consult RV magazines, blogs, and books.
- I will talk to the Motorcoach dealer.
- I will join a group on Reddit.
- I will ask a question on Quora.

Chapter 9

Building Your Success Team

Building your dream life takes effort, but even when you are willing to set the goals and invest the time and energy, you can still face challenges that drain your motivation. Those obstacles might even feel overwhelming, to the point that you aren't sure which choice is the best one. To really stay motivated, you need support and encouragement.

Everyone feels the pressure that comes from pursuing their goals and dreams while dealing with setbacks, obstacles, or difficult circumstances. Leaning on others can give you the perspective and support necessary to stay the course. Later on, as you achieve your goals, you can end up inspiring and supporting others in their journey.

So how can you build a support system, or as I like to call it, your success team? It isn't something that is haphazard, with random individuals. To build success, you need consistency as you deliberately build relationships meant to nurture, motivate, and inspire you to achieve success. These relationships are not anchored in negativity, so your success team isn't going to include individuals who constantly tell you it isn't possible or point out your limitations in a discouraging manner.

The truth is that building your success team starts with you finding individuals who can give you critical feedback, fresh perspectives, and practical assistance. Additionally, your success team needs people who will hold you accountable, serving as a sounding board to keep you on track.

Clearly, there are multiple benefits to building a success team. Let's dive into who should be included and why they can play such a critical role in the success of your second half.

Who Should Be in Your Success Team?

Honestly, the makeup of your success team will depend on what type of dreams and goals you are pursuing. After all, if you want to run your own business, your success team should include other business owners who can mentor you, providing critical advice and the benefit of their experience. It wouldn't benefit you to have a success team made up of people who have never run a business or even worked in leadership roles.

Another point to keep in mind is that your success team is not necessarily going to be a bunch of individuals who are rooting for you and full of positivity. Not that you don't need some of those individuals, but the truth is that you really need people who can give you practical ways to grow into your success and bring your dreams to fruition. You don't have control over what you might struggle with, but instead, focus on what you can control, which includes how you treat yourself and the company you keep.

One of the first parts of building your success team is examining who is already a part of your inner circle. Who provides you with support during the difficult or challenging periods of your life right now?

Typically, they are someone who listens judgment-free, cheers you on, and reminds you of the strengths you already have.

On the other hand, there are those whose primary responses always seem to be fanning your fears, sparking you to worry and stress about the challenges you are facing. Who do you want to have in your life and as a part of your success team?

The truth is that those who might be providing the best support are not necessarily trying to crush your dreams, but they do tend to focus on the obstacles instead of creating solutions. In order to attract those individuals that cheer us on or provide the right kind of support, you need to be one of those individuals yourself.

Awareness involves recognizing that we all need a circle of support that includes the following:

- People who support us in a non-judgmental, honest, and respectful way.
- People who help our creativity flow when we're around them.

The acknowledgment that some topics are off-limits with various individuals because they can focus on the negatives or be a slow leak when it comes to our dreams.

Being a Source of Support for Ourselves

Your support circle isn't going to be made of just one or two individuals. Having lots of people as part of your support circle is key to your success.

Often, the members of your support circle are not all providing the same things. One might provide a listening ear, while another provides support with practical ideas about how to move forward when you are feeling stuck.

While you are pursuing your dreams, your success team might include friends, a partner, colleagues, mentors, or coaches. It doesn't mean you will necessarily be close personal friends and have a close relationship with all of them. Instead, they may just have experience with what you are facing or where you want to take your life.

Here is what supportive people can do to assist you:

- Provide a listening ear as you talk through the situation and sort things out.

- Give you a place to vent when you just need to work through your emotional response.

- Help you to determine what options you have available and the steps to take your dreams to the next level.

Clearly, there are plenty of benefits to growing your support system, especially in terms of the advice and experience you can tap into. But how do you start the process, especially if your dreams are more professional in nature and your close friends and family are not in the same industry or career trajectory?

How to Grow Your Circle of Support

First, don't limit your circle of support or assume that it can only include a definite number. The larger your circle, the greater the chance to achieve your dreams. Your support circle is a foundation, especially when you are taking big risks to propel your life to the next level.

I look back at the support I had from friends to go to Australia. My friend Niki introduced me to an EMT from Australia, who she had observed on her ambulance in Manhattan. My friend Bill introduced me to his brother Glenn, who had the means to go to Australia. My friend Jo-Ann took me to the Windows on the World Restaurant to support me in my interest of going to Australia. The positive support of friends and family helps you feel validated in making the dream a reality.

I will never forget the words of my girlfriend's father, Ray, when I was trying to decide to go to New York to be a paramedic. My girlfriend said, "You won't go. That is too much change to deal with." Ray was talking to me and asked me if I was going to move to New York City. I told him I was not sure if I should go or stay in Massachusetts. Ray said to me, "Steve, you can go and come back if you don't like it. You don't want to be that guy sitting in your chair in your fifties, wondering what it would have been like. Give it a try." Those words were like a giant "on" button being pushed. I was on my way to New York City to be a paramedic. I completed a twenty-five-year career and still live in New York as of the time this book is being printed. Thanks for the advice, Ray.

Before you decide to start growing your circle, think about who will fit and provide the type of support you are looking for. Growing the relationship involves reaching out, inviting them to join you at an event or even for a cup of coffee. I challenge you to take a risk and open the lines of communication with one person, be it someone who you find inspiring or someone who might be a potential mentor. But your circle of support can include life coaches, counselors, and self-help courses. These can help you to achieve your dreams quickly, but with the quality that will ensure the changes you make are long-lasting.

With that in mind, you might want to consider hiring a life coach who can assist you in taking your progress to the next level. You might be reading tons of self-help books, and while their advice makes sense, you might be struggling to figure out how to take their advice and turn it into action. You might also find it easier to break through potential barriers by talking with real people who can serve as a sounding board.

You might like the idea of having someone who can work with you to achieve your dreams and goals. However, if you are looking to work through a multitude of past issues or emotional baggage, a therapist might be the right choice to add to your support circle. A life coach is focused on your future and attaining your goals, which can also make them a critical part of your success team.

With a life coach, you dive into the questions that assist you in identifying what you want in your life, while probing to discover what habits or beliefs could be keeping you from achieving your long-term goals. Together, you become a team that develops an action plan and the attainable steps necessary to bring you closer to your dream life in your second half.

You might know exactly what you should be doing, but it is hard to avoid the distractions and just act. By having a life coach, you have someone to be accountable to and deadlines to meet, which can be critical to keeping you motivated as you work to attain your dreams.

As a coach, I have my clients focus on what they need to do to be successful, providing a level of accountability they might not otherwise have. I also give them encouragement to keep moving forward, particularly with setbacks. I won't tell you what to do, but I am here to help facilitate your goals. While I will challenge your notions of what is possible and what you are capable of achieving, I won't force my ideas on you. When difficult situations arrive, like they always do, then your coach can encourage you to do the things you want to do even if you don't necessarily believe it is possible.

What to Expect in a Typical Coaching Session

The truth is, your coach can be a great way to jump start your second half in a variety of areas. To be clear, you might have to give one area your primary focus before moving on to the next part of your life. With that in mind, you need to be honest as you work with your coach, so they can get a clear idea of where you need to focus your time, energy, and effort. Coaches like to get to know you, so they might have you complete a questionnaire. There could be questions similar to the following:

- What is your vision for the future?
- What motivates you to keep moving forward?
- What do you fear or struggle with?
- What are your greatest successes?
- What are your greatest failures?
- What do you want to change?
- What is going well that you want to keep around?
- What are your priorities?

You might not have all the answers, but the goal is to understand who you are, what you want, and what your vision of the future is. Where do you want to go in this second half? During your coaching sessions, you will speak about what happened since your last session, what your next set of goals is, and what you need to do to achieve them. The conversation will include various tools and resources you can tap into, while also getting effective help through visualization and hypnotherapy.

Here is the important point to remember. None of this works if you aren't willing to put in the effort. Your coach is a critical part of your success team, serving as a cheerleader, sounding board, or even the person who can give you a swift kick in the butt when you need it, but they can't actually make the changes for you. That part is up to you. While they might be able to give you the benefit of their knowledge and experience, only you have the power to implement it into your life.

You are the only one who can actually change your habits, get organized, and stay disciplined enough to follow through. When you show up to your coaching sessions, be honest about where you need help or where you might be struggling to make progress. Then follow through with doing the work between your sessions. If you aren't willing to do the work, then you will gather a lot of ideas, but your life will look the same tomorrow as it does today.

The beauty of having coaching today is that you have the ability to work with your coach in person or online. The benefit of online coaching is that you can work with a variety of people who specialize in multiple areas. Geography doesn't have to be a barrier to connecting with experienced coaches.

Additionally, working with online coaches can help you to have hundreds of coaches to choose from, which can allow you to complete coaching sessions anywhere you happen to be. You can also save time by having coaching sessions in smaller increments versus trying to carve out larger chunks of time to drive to a coaching session. Think of coaching like the gym. Sometimes ease of access can make it simpler for you to incorporate your coaching sessions into your schedule.

How to Choose a Life Coach Effectively

Are your relationships filled with drama and you are struggling to connect with others in a healthy way? Perhaps you want to develop deeper friendships but are not sure how to do that. Your coach could be the person who helps you to dive into this and create a plan of action to improve in this area.

Another area where you might find coaching effective is working on your business acumen. The type of coach you want could be someone who has worked with other business owners and can give you critical advice to help you avoid potential pitfalls or mistakes. The point is that the type of changes you want to make can help you to determine the type of life coach you need.

There are a variety of coaches out there who can be a source of necessary support in multiple professional areas. Other life coaches could be focused on helping you to explore personal growth, including focusing on your strengths, setting meaningful goals, and taking the risks necessary to achieve your dreams.

Here are a few ways to determine if a coach is the right fit for your current needs.

- Do they specialize in your area of need?
- Do they get "you" and what you are trying to achieve?
- Are they local or will you need to use video conferencing?
- Do they fit in with your budget?
- What type of coach do you want to work with?

The synergy between you and your coach is often part of what compels you to keep moving forward successfully. Plus, the beauty of working with life coaches is that over time, as your needs change, you can find another coach to work on a different area of your personal or professional life.

While you want a coach that you can get along with, the most important thing is that you both communicate in a style effective for you, whether you are a visual or auditory learner. When information is presented in a way that makes sense to you, then you can find it easier to implement. If you are feeling raw and vulnerable, your relationship with your coach should serve as a safe place for you to cast off the old you and embrace a new perspective.

Most of the time, your gut will tell you if a coach is a good fit. The goal is to feel comfortable and safe, but also to be challenged by the coach to make necessary changes. Clearly, there are plenty of benefits to working with a coach to achieve great success in your second half. With that in mind, let's talk about how to find satisfaction with your progress, no matter what area you are focusing on.

Steven Kanarian is a highly experienced mentor and leader who is a professional coach. You can e-mail Steve for a free coaching session to discuss building your dreams and suitability to work with him, at Steve.2ndhalfoflife@outlook.com, with the subject "Coaching Session."

Chapter 10

Satisfaction in Achieving Progress

Your second half of life is an amazing time of life. You still have so much time to accomplish your goals and achieve your dreams. Plus, you have a wealth of wisdom and experience to employ as you work toward your goals. My hope is that this book served as inspiration to get the most out of the second half of your life.

Throughout these chapters, my focus was on giving you the tools to help you achieve your dreams and goals. You might have put some aspects of your dreams on pause to raise your family or build your career, but now is the time to push play. Your children are out pursuing their plans and shaping their adult lives. You have the chance to shape the rest of your adult life to be one that brings you joy and satisfaction.

I want to be clear that your focus doesn't have to be on your career. After all, your career is just one part of your life. Be open to exploring what you want to do with other areas of your life, including relationships and discovering or exploring your passions.

That hobby or travel you never had enough time for can take center stage, as time that was devoted to family responsibilities becomes yours again. But to understand how you want to spend your time, it is important to make decisions that align with your values and priorities. At this stage of your life, your priorities need to be front and center. Your second half is not the time to sit back and put your dreams off for another decade or two.

However, we all have picked up a number of bad habits that can impact our choices. People-pleasing, for instance, can negatively influence our dreams, because we put the needs of others in front of what we want to achieve. Part of what I focus on is what habits you might have picked up over the years that could be creating an obstacle to your success at this stage of your life. Develop the habit of doing the hard things and not listening to negativity or criticism.

Exploring your values and beliefs can be a great way to better understand why you make specific decisions and how you can shift your thinking to create different results. Getting out of any rut starts by making decisions and acting in a way that welcomes change.

One of the biggest challenges you might face is being open to change, adapting, and thriving when change happens. For many, the reason they fear change is primarily because of the unknown. What will happen next? What if it doesn't work out right? What if I take a financial loss? How will I recoup that loss?

It is the fear of the unknown and what could go wrong that often leaves individuals stuck in a rut, playing it safe. My goal is to get you to look hard at your fears, what might be holding you back, and give you the ladder to get out of your rut. Manifesting your dreams is possible! The way forward is to make a vision of the way you want to live and move forward, one step at a time.

Throughout this journey to create the amazing second half of your dreams, you will learn so much about yourself. It is the perfect opportunity to explore your talents and dive into what interests you. Embrace your future and all that it has to offer.

Now is the time to seize the day. The choices you make right now are the ones that will shape your future. The truth is that all of us are going to fall asleep in death at some point in the future. When that time comes, you shouldn't be spending your final days buried in regrets. Based on the choices you are making right now, you determine whether you will be in the same place this time next year, or on a completely different path.

It takes a great deal of self-love, discipline, dedication, and determination to live your greatest life. Look within yourself and ask, "Am I living my best life in every area? Am I on course to achieve my dreams? Am I growing personally, mentally, spiritually, and emotionally?" If you aren't, or anything is blocking or preventing that growth, then let it go.

I love vision boards for just this reason. They can be a physical manifestation of your dreams, allowing you to add or remove items as necessary to get your dreams to align with who you are right now, not who you were ten years ago. Once you do the curating of your vision board, take that spirit of curating to the rest of your life. Spend time daily thinking about your dreams, and experience how they feel and affect your senses.

There is something interesting that happens as we get older. We tend to hold on to things, regardless of whether they are beneficial or not. It might be due to sentimentality or because we paid good money for those objects, but the truth is that our lives have started to get cluttered. The counter is full of paper and random objects, and the kitchen has multiple drawers with tools and dishes we never use anymore. Look around your home right now. Is it relaxing or do you feel a lot of pressure and stress? When our homes feel cluttered and it is difficult to move around, our minds can't relax in the space and our stress rises.

Clearly, to achieve your dreams, you need to be able to have a space that contributes to your peace, helps you find joy, or just allows you to relax from the day's activities. That means being discriminatory regarding what deserves to be in your space.

Diving into your second half, you need to do an inventory. What are you holding on to that is no longer working for you? What is draining your time and energy? Adopting the idea of minimalism, for instance, can help you to avoid spending time caring for material possessions instead of what brings you joy and peace.

You have the ability to curate your life by letting go of what no longer serves you, and embracing the things that are meant for you right now in this season of your life. That won't always be easy to do. It might mean letting go of things that take up your time and clutter your physical environment.

When you look at your current space, be honest about what you really need and what is contributing to your mental and physical clutter. Constantly having to deal with clutter detracts us from how we want to spend our time and the relationships we want to deepen and enrich. So be willing to make changes to your environment by reducing your clutter, so you can elevate and highlight those things that contribute to your life in a positive and meaningful way.

On the other hand, you might find that some of your personal or professional relationships do not provide the same level of support, encouragement, or honesty they once did. Curating your life might involve ending these relationships or limiting your interactions with these individuals.

Discipline and emotional self-control are two keys that can propel you forward as you work to achieve your vision. Implementing them can be challenging at times, but it is worth the effort, especially when you have the joy of successfully bringing your dreams into reality.

Finding the Courage to Succeed

Courage is not the absence of fear, but a willingness to keep going despite the fears. Those who display courage face the unknown, refusing to allow worry and fear to keep them from moving forward on their defined path. Your courage also fuels your resilience, since it takes courage to bounce back from challenges or when you deal with an emotionally charged situation.

Diving in and creating your dream life in the second half takes a level of courage that might be challenging to find. This courage is not always a roar. Sometimes it is just your inner voice telling you to try again tomorrow, especially when the day hasn't gone the way you hoped. Failure can be disheartening, especially when it results in a significant setback.

There is a story of a man who went to the circus and asked the elephant trainer, "Why doesn't the elephant pull loose from that stake in the ground he is tied to?" The elephant trainer replied, "The elephant has been tied to that post since it was a small elephant. He has learned that he cannot pull free from that stake. Even though he can clearly pull free now, his mind is conditioned to not even try." Develop the habit of pulling free from misconceptions and limitations you have from your childhood, instead of remaining conditioned to accept your circumstances. You have the power to create change and build the life of your dreams.

With courage, you can learn from failure without letting it define you. That courage will see you through the obstacles, the challenges, and the negativity you will encounter. It is courage that lets you look fear in the face and keep moving forward to create the life you want.

There is also courage necessary when you are faced with circumstances not of your own making. In those moments, you have to decide how you will manage your actions and how you will allow those circumstances to impact your relationships with others. Even when you can't control what is happening, you can control the way you respond to what is happening. It is a powerful place to be when you are able to recognize and implement that level of control.

When we talked about visualizing your dreams, I spent time focusing on how important it is for you to draw a detailed mental picture of your ideal life. The point is that you give it presence in your mind, one that you can reference when you feel that your path might be off-track. The vision board is also a great way to give life to your dreams, allowing you to reset when there are challenges.

Taking Your Vision from Your Mind to Reality

Knowing your dreams and having a clear path to achieve them is just part of your journey. Acting on your goals is what moves you down the path toward a new reality, one that includes your dreams. As a coach, I work with clients to help them map out their goals. We also work on identifying obstacles right away. The greater your understanding of potential obstacles, the better you can come up with a game plan to address them. Attaining your dream is a matter of placing the steppingstones to get you to your destination, taking a step at a time.

Paradigms become apparent as you achieve goals and move on to new ones. You can face your objections, feelings of self-doubt, negativity from family and friends, financial setbacks, and even a lack of the right skill set.

The truth is that your second half doesn't just come with a set of dreams you want to make your reality; you also come with a lot of baggage from the early years of your life. Whether you realize it or not, the baggage from your past can have a powerful impact on your future.

Think about how you grew up and its impact on how you think and make decisions. When you look at your current circumstances, what grabs your attention as being a priority often can trace back to your early experiences. What we do in a coaching session is not therapy where I try to help you unravel your past experiences. Instead, I tend to focus on how you can use those experiences to guide you in this next phase of your life.

Additionally, you might have some habits that are limiting the effectiveness of your actions. During a coaching session, I focus on how you can alter those habits or use them to your advantage. As a coach, my job is to be a cheerleader but also to give you honest feedback. Sometimes, the best way to stay on track is to have someone who holds us accountable.

Every coaching session involves talking about successes you have had, setting goals, and being held accountable to reach your goal. You might find that some of those things that were undone are no longer worth pursuing. On the other hand, you might find that you now can focus on those previously undone tasks, now that others have been completed.

The point of coaching is to receive the support you need to achieve your dreams. As goals are completed, you will likely find that your life is aligning more with your vision. While that is an exciting time, you might find your dreams begin to change. That leaves you with a new set of goals and a fresh path forward.

Finding Joy and Peace Where You Are

At this point, when your second half aligns with your vision, you might feel driven to find the next set of goals or to take the next set of actions for your latest dream. However, I also want you to remember that you need to stop and enjoy what you have accomplished.

Your heart can be joyful as you live in a way that brings you peace and contentment. But your life isn't just full of what you accomplish; it is also enriched by the relationships that you create and allow to deepen with time. In the moments when you are struggling with obstacles or difficult circumstances, those relationships can prove to be a vital source of support.

The truth is that your second half can be full of amazing moments, but there are also going to be moments of painful loss. My children are adults now, and my parents have aged considerably. You might be in the same position, as older loved ones require more care and difficult decisions come up. Your health might also take a turn, leaving you wondering if your dream life is even possible.

I want to be clear that these are challenges we all face at one point or another. We all deal with loss, particularly as we get older. I want you to remember that you have the chance to make the most of the time given to you on this earth. Our loved ones might leave this earth, but they stay with us in our minds and hearts. As you achieve your dreams, take them with you. It can add a deeper meaning when you accomplish a new goal or see the results of your hard work.

I am reminded of what it is like to climb a mountain. Sherpas serve as guides, helping others to reach their destinations, encouraging them when necessary, and giving critical feedback in other instances. Perhaps achieving your dreams in the second half feels as if you are trying to climb a mountain. First, it is important to recognize the progress you have made in many areas of your life. Give yourself credit for what you have already achieved.

Second, find a guide to help you in this next stage. It might be a coach or mentor, but by doing so, you create an opportunity to build upon what you have already done. Finding your sherpa to guide your way is critical to having a successful second half. Never stop focusing on what you can accomplish, or on bringing your dreams into reality. There is a joy that comes with working together to attain your vision.

If you are ready to step into your second half, now is the time. With the right coach and plan of action, you can achieve the life you have always dreamed of. By using the steps outlined here, you can get started right now and stop pushing off until tomorrow what is possible today!

About the Author

Steven Kanarian is an author, life coach, and entrepreneur. He also served as a first responder in New York City for twenty-five years. Steven currently lives on the East Coast, where he continues to provide expert coaching to individuals for their personal and professional lives.

He is a certified life coach who strives to share his experience and teaching skills with others to enhance their lives and fulfill their goals. Steven has a Master of Public Health from New York Medical College, School of Public Health. He has taught at major New York colleges and hospitals.

As a paramedic and lieutenant with the FDNY, Steve is a September 11, 2001 rescuer. He also has extensive experience with helping people endure adversity. Steven has been a guiding light to many who benefitted from his guidance and insight. Steven always helps people to excel and reach their full potential.

He is also the author of *The Downwind Walk: A USAR Paramedic's Experiences on September 11, 2001,* available on Amazon.com.

With over 30 years of experience as an educator and leader, Steve is available for coaching on health, career, and goal-centered dreams you may have. Email Steve at **Steve.2ndhalfoflife@outlook.com** and use the subject line, "I'm ready, Steve."

Made in the USA
Middletown, DE
04 November 2024

63524649R00070